Economic Benefits to Local Communities from National Park Visitation and Payroll, 2009

Natural Resource Report NPS/NRPC/SSD/NRR—2011/281

Daniel J. Stynes

Department of Community, Agriculture, Recreation and Resource Studies
Michigan State University
East Lansing, Michigan 48824-1222

January 2011

U.S. Department of the Interior
National Park Service
Natural Resource Program Center
Fort Collins, Colorado

The National Park Service, Natural Resource Program Center publishes a range of reports that address natural resource topics of interest and applicability to a broad audience in the National Park Service and others in natural resource management, including scientists, conservation and environmental constituencies, and the public.

The Natural Resource Report Series is used to disseminate high-priority, current natural resource management information with managerial application. The series targets a general, diverse audience, and may contain NPS policy considerations or address sensitive issues of management applicability.

All manuscripts in the series receive the appropriate level of peer review to ensure that the information is scientifically credible, technically accurate, appropriately written for the intended audience, and designed and published in a professional manner.

This report received formal peer review by subject-matter experts who were not directly involved in the collection, analysis, or reporting of the data, and whose background and expertise put them on par technically and scientifically with the authors of the information.

Views, statements, findings, conclusions, recommendations, and data in this report do not necessarily reflect views and policies of the National Park Service, U.S. Department of the Interior. Mention of trade names or commercial products does not constitute endorsement or recommendation for use by the U.S. Government.

This report is available from the Social Science Division (www.nature.nps.gov/socialscience/index.cfm) and the Natural Resource Publications Management website (http://www.nature.nps.gov/publications/NRPM).

Please cite this publication as:

Stynes, D. J. 2011. Economic benefits to local communities from national park visitation and payroll, 2009. Natural Resource Report NPS/NRPC/SSD/NRR—2011/281. National Park Service, Fort Collins, Colorado.

NPS 999/106327, January 2011

Contents

	Page
Figures and Tables	iv
Executive Summary	v
Introduction	1
2009 Updates	1
Recreation Visits	2
Visitor Spending	3
Local Impacts of Visitor Spending	4
Economic Significance	6
Economic Impacts	6
National Economic Significance of NPS Visitor Spending	7
Impacts of NPS Payrolls	8
State-by-State Impact Estimates	9
Methods	9
Errors and Limitations	11
References	15
Appendices	17

Figures and Tables

Page

Figure 1. Distribution of National Park Visitor Spending 4

Table 1. National Park Visitor Spending in the Local Area by Segment, 2009 3
Table 2. National Park Visitor Spending by Segment, 2009 4
Table 3. Economic Significance of National Park Visitor Spending to Local Economies, 2009 5
Table 4. Economic Impacts of National Park Visitor Spending on Local Economies, 2009 5
Table 5. Economic Significance of National Park Visitor Spending on National Economy, 2009 7
Table 6. NPS Payroll Impacts on Local Economies, 2009 8
Table 7. Combined Impacts on Local Economies–Visitor Spending and Payroll 9

Executive Summary

The National Park System received 285.6 million recreation visits in 2009. Park visitors spent $11.89 billion in local gateway regions (within roughly 60 miles of the park). Visitors staying outside the park in motels, hotels, cabins and bed and breakfasts accounted for 56% of the total spending. Over half of the spending was for lodging and meals, 15% for gas and local transportation, 9% for groceries, and 14% for other retail purchases.

The contribution of this spending to the national economy is 247,000 jobs, $9.15 billion in labor income, and $15.58 billion in value added[1]. The direct effects of visitor spending are at the local level in gateway regions around national parks. Local economic impacts were estimated after excluding spending by visitors from the local area (9.7% of the total). Combining local impacts across all parks yields a total local impact including direct and secondary effects of 149,500 jobs, $4.32 billion in labor income, and $7.33 billion value added. The four local economic sectors most directly affected by non-local visitor spending are lodging, restaurants, retail trade, and amusements. Visitor spending supports 44,000 jobs in restaurants and bars, 37,600 jobs in lodging establishments, almost 20,000 jobs in retail and wholesale trade, and 8,600 jobs in amusements.

Parks also impact the local region through the NPS payroll. In Fiscal Year 2009 the National Park Service employed 26,121 people with a total payroll of $1,618 million in wages, salaries, and payroll benefits. Including the induced effects of the spending of NPS wages and salaries in the local region, the total local economic impacts of park payrolls are $2.32 billion in labor income, $2.52 billion in value added, and 38,175 jobs (including NPS jobs).

---

[1] National estimates use IMPLAN multipliers for the U.S. economy. These are larger than estimates in the 2008 report (Stynes, 2009) where national estimates were reported as the sum of impacts on local economies.

Introduction

This report provides updated estimates of National Park Service (NPS) visitor spending for 2009 and estimates the economic impacts of visitor spending and the NPS payroll on local economies. Visitor spending and impacts are estimated using the Money Generation Model version 2 (MGM2) model (Stynes et. al. 2000) based on calendar year 2009 park visits, spending averages from park visitor surveys, and local area economic multipliers. Impacts of the NPS payroll are estimated based on fiscal year (FY) 2009 payroll data for each park.

Visitor spending impacts are estimated for all park units with visitation data. Payroll impacts are estimated for all parks including administrative units and parks without visit count data. Impacts measure the direct and secondary effects of visitor spending and park payrolls in terms of jobs, income, and value added.[2] Direct effects cover businesses selling goods and services directly to park visitors. Secondary effects include indirect effects resulting from sales to backward-linked industries within the local region and induced effects from household spending of income earned directly or indirectly from visitor spending. Impacts of construction activity and park purchases of goods and services are not included.

Impacts are estimated at both the national and local level. Most spending directly associated with park visits occurs in gateway regions around each park. Impacts of this spending on the local economies are estimated using local input-output models for each park. Local regions are defined as a 60-mile radius[3] around each park. To estimate impacts on the national economy, spending within roughly 60 miles of the park is applied to the national input-output model. System-wide totals covering impacts on local economies are also estimated by summing the spending and local impact estimates for all park units. Results for individual park units are reported in the Appendix.

2009 Updates

The 2009 estimates reflect new visitor surveys at ten parks. In 2008/2009 visitor surveys were conducted at Everglades NP, Fort Larned NHS, Grand Teton NP, Homestead NM of America, James A. Garfield NHS, Minuteman Missile NHS, Perry's Victory and International Peace Memorial, Sleeping Bear Dunes NL, Women's Rights NHP, and Yosemite NP.[4] New visitor spending and impact estimates were also developed for Denali NP (Stynes and Ackerman 2010). Spending and visitor profiles for these parks were updated based upon the survey data. For other parks, spending profiles from 2008 were price adjusted to 2009 using Bureau of Labor Statistics

---

[2] Jobs include full-time and part-time jobs. Seasonal positions are adjusted to an annual basis. Labor income covers wages and salaries, including income of sole proprietors and payroll benefits. Value added is the sum of labor income, profits and rents, and indirect business taxes. It can also be defined as total sales net of the costs of all non-labor inputs. Value added is the preferred economic measure of the contribution of an industry or activity to the economy.

[3] The 60-mile radius is a general average representing the primary impact region around most parks. The radius is closer to 30 miles for parks in urban settings and as large as 100 miles for some western parks. Economic multipliers are based on regions defined as groupings of counties to approximate a 60-mile radius of the park.

[4] These studies are conducted by the Visitor Services Project (VSP) at the University of Idaho. Reports for individual parks are available at their website: http://www.psu.uidaho.edu/vsp.reports.htm

consumer price indices for each spending category. Consumer prices remained fairly stable between 2008 and 2009 except for a drop of 7% in lodging and a 27% drop in fuel prices. Visit and overnight stay figures for all parks were updated to 2009 (NPS 2010).

Multipliers for all parks were re-estimated using IMPLAN version 3.0 and 2008 county economic data. Local regions were defined to include all counties within 60 road miles of each park. Estimates in previous years for most parks were based on "generic multipliers" derived from input-output models estimated with IMPLAN using 2001 county-level data. Distinct multipliers for local regions were based on the population of the region. Job estimates were adjusted for price changes over time using the general consumer price index.

Multipliers are based on IMPLAN's trade flow models. This change is an improvement over the econometric models in version 2.0 and will alter estimates of secondary effects for local regions. The updated employment multipliers using 2008 data are on average about 30% lower than previous estimates using MGM2 generic multipliers that were based on IMPLAN version 2.0. Lower job to sales ratios for most sectors reflect significant structural changes in the U.S. economy since 2001. In most cases, reductions in the number of jobs to produce a given level of output were greater than what would be expected just from price changes.

Recreation Visits

The National Park System received 285.6 million recreation visits in 2009. Visitor spending was estimated by dividing visitors to each park into segments with distinct spending patterns and applying spending averages based on surveys of park visitors at selected parks. As spending averages are measured on a party day basis (party nights for overnight trips), the NPS counts of recreation visits are converted from person entries to a park to party days in the area by applying average party size, length of stay, and park re-entry factors. This adjusts for some double counting of visits. To the extent possible, spending not directly related to a park visit is excluded.[5]

In 2009 there were 14.59 million recreation overnight stays in the parks, representing 3.4% of all visits. Twenty-nine percent of park visits were day trips by local residents, 41% were day trips from 60 miles or more,[6] and 30% involved an overnight stay near the park. Visitor spending depends on the number of days spent in the local area and also the type of lodging on overnight trips. Non-local day trips account for 34% of the party days spent in the local area, local day trips 28%, and overnight stays 38%. Sixty-five percent of all overnight stays by park visitors are in motels, lodges, or bed and breakfasts outside the park; another 18% are in campgrounds outside the park; and 12% are inside the park in NPS campgrounds, lodges, or backcountry sites.

---

[5] For example, spending during extended stays in an area visiting relatives, on business, or when the park visit was not the primary trip purpose is excluded. For most historic sites and parks in urban areas, spending for one day or night is counted for each park entry. Where several park units are within a 60-mile radius, adjustments are made for those visiting more than one park on the same day.

[6] Day trips include pass-thru visitors not spending a night within 60 miles of the park as well as stays with friends and relatives and in owned seasonal homes.

Visitor Spending

Visitor spending averages cover expenses within the local region, excluding park entry fees. Spending averages for each segment are derived from park visitor surveys at selected parks over the past nine years. Bureau of Labor Statistics price indices for each spending category are applied to adjust all spending to 2009 dollars.

NPS System-wide spending averages for 2009 are given in Table 1 for seven distinct visitor segments. A typical park visitor party on a day trip spends $39 if a local resident and $66 if non-local (Table 1).

Table 1. National Park Visitor Spending in the Local Area by Segment, 2009 ($ per party per day/night)

Spending category	Visitor Segment						
	Local Day Trip	Non-local Day Trip	NPS Lodge	NPS Camp Ground	Back-country	Motel-Outside Park	Camp-Outside Park
Motel, hotel, B&B	0.00	0.00	156.63	0.00	5.88	101.31	0.00
Camping fees	0.00	0.00	0.00	20.48	2.61	0.00	25.54
Restaurants & bars	13.05	20.38	78.26	15.09	8.71	67.76	16.42
Amusements	4.13	8.46	24.39	8.58	4.58	20.61	16.87
Groceries	6.28	7.35	13.04	18.87	6.01	16.84	11.85
Gas & oil	6.45	15.11	22.00	19.68	11.92	17.04	17.85
Local transportation	0.51	1.20	4.37	1.43	0.61	3.39	1.29
Retail Purchases	8.23	13.53	32.46	12.82	12.23	29.44	22.22
Total	38.66	66.04	331.16	96.94	52.56	256.38	112.05

On a party night basis, spending by visitors on overnight trips varies from $52 for backcountry campers to $331 for visitors staying in park lodges. Campers spend $112 per night if staying outside the park and $97 if staying inside the park. Spending averages at individual parks vary from these System-wide averages due to differences in local prices and spending opportunities. For example, while non-local visitors on day trips spent $37 per party at Badlands NP in 2009, their counterparts at Grand Canyon spent $140.

In total, park visitors spent $11.89 billion in the local region surrounding the parks in 2009.[7] Local residents account for 9.7% of this spending (Table 2). Visitors staying in motels and lodges outside the park account for 56% of the total spending while non-local visitors on day trips contribute 20% of all spending.

Lodging and restaurant/bar expenses each account for about a quarter of the spending. Transportation expenses (mainly auto fuel) account for 15%, groceries 9%, other retail purchases 14%, and recreation and entertainment 10% (Figure 1).

---

[7] Spending figures exclude airfares and other trip spending beyond 60 miles of the park. Purchases of durable goods (boats, RVs) and major equipment are also excluded. Special expenses for commercial rafting trips, air overflights and other special activities are not fully captured for all parks.

Table 2. National Park Visitor Spending by Segment, 2009

Segment	Total Spending ($ Millions)	Percent of Spending
Local Day Trip	1,152	9.7%
Non-local Day Trip	2,387	20.1%
Lodge/Cabin-In Park	393	3.3%
Camp-In Park	277	2.3%
Backcountry Campers	33	0.3%
Motel-Outside Park	6,673	56.1%
Camp-Outside Park	789	6.6%
Other Overnight Visitors	190	1.6%
Total	**11,893**	**100%**

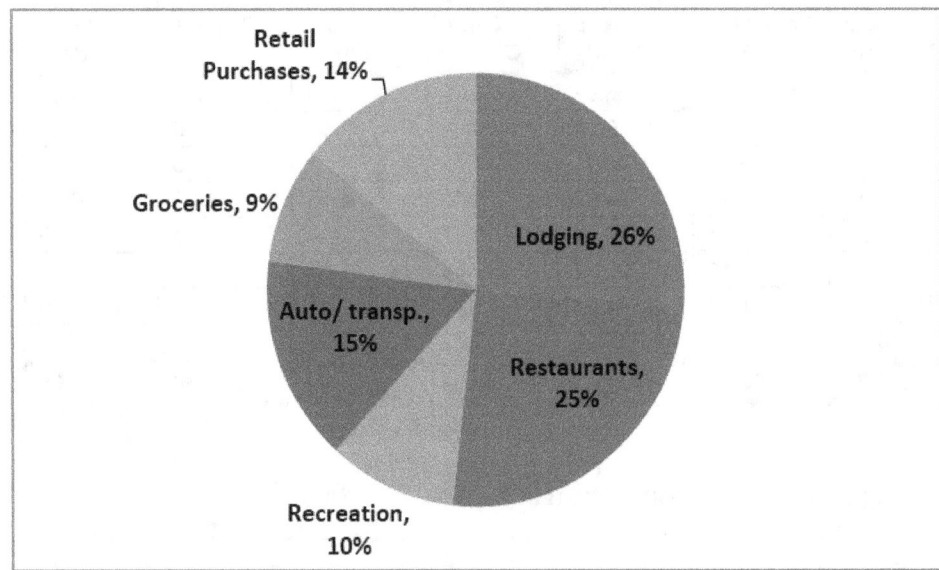

Figure 1. Distribution of National Park Visitor Spending

Local Impacts of Visitor Spending

Local economic impacts of visitor spending are estimated in the MGM2 model using multipliers for local areas around each park. Multipliers capture both the direct and secondary economic effects in gateway communities around the parks in terms of jobs, labor income, and value added. National totals are calculated as the sum of the local impacts for 356 park units that have counts of visitors.

Both economic significance and economic impacts were estimated. The economic significance estimates in Table 3 measure the impacts of all visitor spending ($11.89 billion), including that of local visitors. Economic impacts in Table 4 exclude spending by local visitors, estimating the impacts of the $10.74 billion spent by visitors who do not reside within the local region.

Table 3. Economic Significance of National Park Visitor Spending to Local Economies, 2009

Sector/Spending category	Sales ($ Millions)	Jobs	Labor Income ($ Millions)	Value Added ($ Millions)
Direct Effects				
Motel, hotel cabin or B&B	2,897	34,711	984	1,791
Camping fees	239	2,871	71	126
Restaurants & bars	3,031	50,146	1,068	1,580
Amusements & Entertain.	1,185	9,632	258	449
Other vehicle expenses	136	1,623	51	76
Local transportation	270	5,235	107	153
Grocery stores	260	4,236	110	169
Gas stations	315	3,413	96	218
Other retail	808	13,936	354	528
Wholesale Trade	280	1,535	106	182
Local Manufacturing.	235	477	31	41
Total Direct Effects	9,657	127,814	3,237	5,313
Secondary Effects	4,725	35,670	1,528	2,752
Total Effects	**14,382**	**163,483**	**4,765**	**8,065**

Notes: Economic significance covers all $11.89 billion in spending of park visitors in the local region, including that of local visitors. Jobs include full-time and part-time jobs with seasonal positions adjusted to an annual basis. Labor income covers wages and salaries, including income of sole proprietors and payroll benefits. Value added is the sum of labor income, profits and rents, and indirect business taxes.

Table 4. Economic Impacts of National Park Visitor Spending on Local Economies, 2009

Sector/Spending category	Sales ($ Millions)	Jobs	Labor Income ($ Millions)	Value Added ($ Millions)
Direct Effects				
Motel, hotel cabin or B&B	2,897	34,711	984	1,791
Camping fees	239	2,871	71	126
Restaurants & bars	2,647	44,040	930	1,376
Amusements & Entertain.	1,057	8,629	231	400
Other vehicle expenses	122	1,463	46	68
Local transportation	268	5,192	107	152
Grocery stores	213	3,506	90	138
Gas stations	271	2,971	82	187
Other retail	693	12,002	304	453
Wholesale Trade	231	1,292	87	150
Local Manufacturing	176	361	23	31
Total Direct Effects	8,817	117,038	2,955	4,872
Secondary Effects	4,232	32,425	1,367	2,460
Total Effects	**13,048**	**149,463**	**4,321**	**7,332**

Note: Economic impacts cover the $10.74 billion spent by non-local visitors.

Economic impact measures attempt to estimate the likely losses in economic activity to the region in the absence of the park. Should the park opportunities not be available, it is assumed that local residents would spend the money on other local activities, while visitors from outside the region would not have made a trip to the region.[8] Spending by local residents on visits to the park do not represent "new money" to the region and are therefore generally excluded when estimating impacts. Local resident spending is included in the economic significance measures, as these capture all economic activity associated with park visits, including local and non-local visitors.

Economic Significance

The $11.89 billion spent by park visitors within 60 miles of the park (Table 2) has a total economic effect (significance) of $14.4 billion in sales, $4.8 billion in labor income, and $8.0 billion in value added. Visitor spending supports about 163,500 jobs in gateway regions. Total effects may be divided between the direct effects that occur in businesses selling goods and services directly to park visitors and secondary effects that result from the circulation of this money within the local economy.[9]

Direct effects are $9.66 billion in sales, $3.24 billion in labor income, $5.31 billion in value added, and 128,000 jobs. The local region captures 81% of all visitor spending as direct sales. Note that direct sales of $9.66 billion is less than the $11.89 billion in visitor spending as most of the manufacturing share of retail purchases (groceries, gas, sporting goods, souvenirs) is not included. It is assumed that most of the producer price of retail purchases immediately leaks out of the region to cover the cost of goods sold. Sales figures for retail and wholesale trade are the margins on retail purchases.

The average sales multiplier across all local park regions is 1.49. For every dollar of direct sales another $.49 in sales is generated in the local region through secondary effects.

Economic Impacts

Excluding $1.15 billion dollars spent by local residents on park visits reduces the total spending to $10.74 billion (Table 2) for the impact analysis. Local visitors represent about 29% of all visits but less than 10% of all visitor spending. The total effects of visitor spending excluding locals is $13.05 billion in sales, $4.32 billion in labor income, $7.33 billion in value added, and 149,500 jobs. The economic sectors most directly affected are lodging, restaurants, retail trade, and amusements. Visitor spending supports almost 44,000 jobs in restaurants and bars, 37,600 jobs in lodging sectors, almost 20,000 jobs in retail and wholesale trade, and 8,600 jobs in amusements.

---

[8] To the extent possible, spending not directly associated with a park visit is also excluded. For example, only one night's expenses are counted for visitors in the area primarily on business, visiting relatives, or visiting other attractions. For parks with visitor surveys, spending attributed to a park visit was estimated based on the percentage of visitors identifying the park visit as the primary purpose of the trip.

[9] Secondary effects include indirect effects of businesses buying goods and services from backward-linked local firms and induced effects of household spending of their earnings.

National Economic Significance of NPS Visitor Spending

The contribution of NPS visitor spending to the national economy can be estimated by applying the spending totals to multipliers for the national economy. This circulates spending that occurs within gateway regions around national parks within the broader national economy, capturing impacts on sectors that manufacture goods purchased by park visitors and additional secondary effects.

The estimates do not include spending by park visitors at home for durable goods such as camping, hunting and fishing equipment, recreation vehicles, boats, and other goods used on trips to the national parks. The estimates also exclude airfares and other en route spending that occurs more than 60 miles from the park. Since many long-distance trips involve multiple purposes and often visits to multiple parks, it is difficult to capture these expenses without double counting or attributing spending not directly related to a national park visit.

With the above exclusions, the contribution of visitor spending to the national economy is 247,000 jobs, $9.15 billion in labor income, and $15.58 billion in value added (Table 5)[10]. With the exception of manufacturing activity and a portion of activity in wholesale trade, the direct effects of visitor spending accrue to local regions around national parks.[11]

Compared to the contribution to local economies (Table 4), an additional 83,500 jobs are supported nationally by NPS visitor spending, primarily due to the greater indirect and induced effects at the national level. The sales multiplier for NPS visitor spending at the national level is 2.68, compared to an average of 1.49 for local regions around national parks.

Table 5. Economic Significance of National Park Visitor Spending on National Economy, 2009

Sector/Spending category	Sales ($ Millions)	Jobs	Labor Income ($ Millions)	Value Added ($ Millions)
Direct Effects				
Motel, hotel, cabin or B&B	2,897	34,711	984	1,791
Camping fees	239	2,871	71	126
Restaurants & bars	3,031	50,146	1,068	1,580
Amusements & Entertain.	1,185	9,632	258	449
Other vehicle expenses	136	1,623	51	76
Local transportation	270	5,235	107	153
Grocery stores	260	4,236	110	169
Gas stations	315	3,413	96	218
Other retail	808	13,936	354	528
Wholesale Trade	450	2,209	171	294
Local Manufacturing	1,722	3,842	254	337
Total Direct Effects	11,314	131,852	3,525	5,721
Secondary Effects	19,077	115,104	5,627	9,863
Total Effects	**30,391**	**246,956**	**9,152**	**15,584**

---

[10] These estimates use national multipliers to estimate secondary effects. This is a change from the 2008 report where national economic effects were estimated as the sum of local impacts using local area multipliers.
[11] Local economic ratios are therefore used to estimate the direct effects. National multipliers are used to estimate secondary effects. With the exception of wholesale trade and manufacturing sectors, the national direct effects (Table 5) are therefore the same as the local direct effects (Table 4).

Impacts of NPS Payrolls

National park units also impact local economies through their own spending, especially NPS payrolls. Payroll impacts were estimated for FY 2009. In FY 2009 the National Park Service employed 26,121 people[12] with a total payroll of $1,618 million in wages, salaries, and payroll benefits (Table 6). Induced effects of the NPS payroll were estimated using multipliers for IMPLAN sector 439 (federal government payroll), with an adjustment for a share that IMPLAN assigns to capital depreciation. Including the induced effects of the spending of NPS wages and salaries in the local region, the total local economic impact of park payrolls in 2009 was $2.32 billion in labor income, $2.52 billion in value added, and 38,175 jobs.

Table 6. NPS Payroll Impacts on Local Economies, 2009

	Jobs	Labor Income ($ Millions)	Value Added ($ Millions)
NPS Payroll	26,121	1,618	1,618
Induced Effects	12,053	698	899
Total Local impacts	**38,175**	**2,316**	**2,517**

Impacts of park payrolls for each park unit were estimated by applying economic multipliers to wage and salary data to capture the induced effects of NPS employee spending on local economies. The overall employment multiplier for NPS jobs is 1.46. For every two NPS jobs, another local job is supported through the induced effects of employee spending in the local region. There are additional local economic effects from NPS purchases of goods and services from local suppliers and from construction activity. These impacts were not estimated.

The visitor spending and payroll impacts may be combined, as park admission fees and most other visitor spending accruing to the National Park Service were omitted from the visitor spending figures to avoid double counting.[13] Using the visitor spending impact estimates from Table 4, which exclude spending of local visitors, the combined total impacts including secondary effects are $6.64 billion in labor income, $9.85 billion in value added, and 187,600 local jobs. Visitor spending accounts for 80% of the total jobs and 74% of the total value added (Table 7).

---

[12] The number of employees is estimated as an annual average for each park, so that seasonal positions are converted to annual equivalents. However, the job estimates include both full-time and part-time positions.
[13] There will be some double counting of camping fees as payments to concessionaires could not be fully sorted out from payments to the National Park Service.

Table 7. Combined Impacts on Local Economies–Visitor Spending and Payroll

Impact Measure	Visitor Spending Impacts[a]	NPS Payroll Impacts	Combined Impacts	Visitor Spending Share
Direct Effects				
Jobs	117,038	26,121	143,159	82%
Labor Income ($ Millions)	$2,955	$1,618	4,573	65%
Value Added ($ Millions)	$4,872	$1,618	6,490	75%
Total Effects				
Jobs	149,463	38,175	187,637	80%
Labor Income ($ Millions)	$4,321	$2,316	6,637	65%
Value Added ($ Millions)	$7,332	$2,517	9,849	74%

[a] Excludes spending by local visitors

State-by-State Impact Estimates

Economic impacts of individual parks can be aggregated to the state level with a few complications. While most parks fall within a single state, there are 20 park units with facilities in more than one state. For these parks, shares of visits were assigned to each state based on percentages provided by the NPS Public Use Statistics Office. It was assumed that spending and economic impacts are proportional to where recreation visits are assigned.

Estimates of recreation visits, spending, and local economic impacts for each state and U.S. territory are given in Table A-4 in the Appendix. States receiving the greatest economic effects from NPS visitor and payroll spending are Washington, D.C.; California; Arizona; North Carolina; Virginia; and Utah. Regional totals are given in Table A-5.

It should be noted that the state and regional totals represent an accumulation of local impacts within roughly 60 miles of each park. The total economic effects on each state or region would be much larger if we included all spending of NPS visitors within each state and used statewide multipliers instead of local ones to capture the secondary effects. As noted earlier, impacts reported here do not include long-distance travel, airfares, or purchases made at home for items that may be used on trips to national parks.

Methods

Spending and impacts were estimated using the MGM2. NPS public use statistics for calendar year 2009 provide estimates of the number of recreation visits and overnight stays at each park. For each park, recreation visits were allocated to the seven MGM2 segments,[14] converted to party days/nights spent in the local area and then multiplied by per-day spending averages for each segment. Spending and impact estimates for 2009 are made individually for each park unit

---

[14] Visits are classified as local day trips, non-local day trips, and overnight trips staying in campgrounds or hotels, lodges, cabins, and bed and breakfasts. For parks with lodging facilities within the park, visitors staying in park lodges, campgrounds, or backcountry sites are distinguished from those staying outside the park in motels or non-NPS campgrounds. Visitors staying with friends or relatives, in owned seasonal homes, or passing through without a local overnight stay are generally treated as day trips.

and then summed to obtain national totals for impacts on local regions. Impacts on the national economy are also estimated by applying all visitor spending to multipliers for the national economy.

Spending averages cover all trip expenses within roughly 60 miles of the park. They therefore exclude most en route expenses on longer trips, as well as airfares and purchases made at home in preparation for the trip, including costs of durable goods and equipment. Spending averages vary from park to park based on the type of park and the regional setting (low, medium, or high spending area).

The segment mix is very important in estimating visitor spending, as spending varies considerably across the MGM2 segments. Segment shares are estimated based on park overnight stay data and, where available, park visitor surveys. For park units that lack recent visitor surveys, estimates are made by generalizing from studies at similar parks or based on manager or researcher judgment.

For parks with VSP (Visitor Services Project) studies over the past nine years, spending averages are estimated from the visitor survey data at each park.[15] Averages estimated in the surveys were price adjusted to 2009 using BLS price indices for each spending category. Sampling errors for the spending averages in VSP studies are generally 5–10% overall and can be as high as 20% for individual visitor segments.

The observed spending patterns in park visitor studies are then used to estimate spending averages for other parks that lack visitor spending surveys. This procedure will not capture some spending variations attributable to unique characteristics of a given park or gateway region—for example, the wider use of public transportation at Alaska parks or extra expenses for special commercial attractions in or around some parks, such as rafting trips, air overflights, and other tours. When visitor studies are conducted at individual parks, these unique situations are taken into account. For example, river runners were treated as a distinct segment at Grand Canyon National Park (Stynes and Sun 2005).

Multipliers for local regions around national parks were applied to the spending totals to translate spending into jobs, income, and value added and also to estimate secondary effects. All MGM2 multipliers were re-estimated this year using IMPLAN ver 3.0 and 2008 economic data (Minnesota IMPLAN Group 2010).

With the exception of parks with new visitor surveys in 2008 or 2009, no changes were made in party sizes, lengths of stay, or re-entry factors between 2008 and 2009. MGM2 model parameters for individual parks are adjusted over time as new park visitor studies are conducted or other relevant information becomes available.

Impacts of park payrolls were estimated for each park by applying local area multipliers to NPS wage and salary figures for FY 2009. Multipliers capture the induced effects of park employee spending by re-circulating their income as household spending within the local economy. Payroll

---

[15] Detailed impact reports for parks that have included economic questions in their VSP studies are available at the MGM2 (http://web4.canr.msu.edu/mgm2/) or NPS social science websites (http://www.nature.nps.gov/socialscience/products.cfm#MGM2Reports).

benefits were not re-circulated in estimating secondary effects of park employee spending, but the direct payroll benefits are included in total value added. Multipliers for IMPLAN sector 439 (federal government payroll) were applied to wages and salaries at each park to estimate induced effects.[16] Local impacts of park purchases of supplies and services or construction activities were not included in the analysis.

The number of employees for each park was estimated by totaling the number of distinct social security numbers in each pay period and dividing by the number of pay periods. The figure is therefore an annual average. Four seasonal jobs for three months count as one job. No distinction is made between part-time and full-time employees. Jobs, salary, and payroll benefits are assigned to the park where the employee's time was charged, which may differ from their duty station.

Spending and impact totals for states were developed from the 2009 estimates by summing the results for all units in a given state using the mailing address for the park to identify the state. Twenty parks have facilities in more than one state. For these parks, visitors and spending were allocated to individual states based on shares used by the NPS Public Use Statistics Office for allocating visits to states. For example, visits to Great Smoky Mountains NP were split 44% to North Carolina and 56% to Tennessee. It should be noted that these allocations may not fully account for where the spending and impacts occur. There are also many other parks with facilities in a single state but located within 60 miles of a state border. A portion of the spending and impacts for these parks may accrue to nearby states. For example, the local region for Saint-Gaudens NHS includes counties in both Vermont and New Hampshire (Stynes 2008), but all impacts in this report are assigned to New Hampshire since the visitor surveys do not identify exactly where spending may have occurred within the local region.

Errors and Limitations

The accuracy of the spending and impact estimates rests largely on the input data, namely (1) public use recreation visit and overnight stay data; (2) party size, length of stay, and park re-entry conversion factors; (3) visitor segment shares; (4) spending averages; and (5) local area multipliers.

Public use data provides reasonably accurate estimates of visitor entries for most parks. Some visitors may be missed by the counting procedures, while others may be counted multiple times when they re-enter a park more than once on a single trip. Accurate estimates of park re-entries, party sizes, and lengths of stay in the area are needed to convert park entries to the number of visitor or party days in the region. Visitors staying overnight outside the park pose significant problems as they tend to be the greatest spenders and may enter the park several times during their stay. Similarly, visitors staying inside the park may enter and leave several times during their stay and be counted each time as a distinct visit. Re-entry factors adjust for these problems to the extent possible.

---

[16] Multipliers were adjusted by a factor of 1.1359 to account for the share of federal payroll that IMPLAN assigns to capital depreciation.

For multi-purpose trips, it is difficult to determine what portion of the spending should be attributed to the park visit. This is especially a problem for historic sites and parks in urban areas or parks in multiple-attraction destinations. For parks with visitor surveys, the proportion of days and spending counted was decided based on stated trip purposes and the importance of the park in generating the trip to the region.

Parkways and urban parks pose special difficulties for economic impact analyses. These units have some of the highest number of visits while posing the most difficult problems for estimating visits, spending, and impacts. The majority of visits to these types of units were assumed to be local or non-local day trips, and only one night of spending was counted for overnight trips. Due to the high numbers of visits at these units, small changes in assumed spending averages or segment mixes can swing the spending estimates by substantial amounts.

Clusters of parks within a single 60-mile area pose additional difficulties. For example, the many monuments and parks in the Washington, D.C., area each count visitors separately. Similar difficulties exist for clusters of parks in Boston, New York, and San Francisco. To avoid double counting of spending across many national capital parks, we must know how many times a visitor has been counted at park units during a trip to the Washington, D.C., area. For parks in the National Capital Region, we currently assume an average of 1.7 park visits are counted for local day trips, 3.4 visits for non-local day trips, and 5.1 park visits on overnight trips. The non-local visitor spending total for the National Capital Region in 2009 was $1.17 billion. This is 14% of the Travel Industry Association tourist spending estimate of $8.3 billion for Washington, D.C., in 2008 (USTA 2010).

NPS units in Alaska also pose special problems for economic analysis. Spending opportunities near Alaska parks are limited and for many visitors the park visit is part of a cruise or guided tour, frequently purchased as a package. Most visitors are on extended trips to Alaska, making it difficult to allocate expenses to a particular park visit. Lodging, vehicle rentals, and air expenses frequently occur in Anchorage, many miles from the park. Also, many Alaska parks are only accessible by air or boat, so spending profiles estimated from visitor surveys at parks in the lower 48 states do not apply well. Due to the prominence of cruise lines and package tours, special studies are required to estimate the proportion of visitor spending that stays in the local regions around national park units in Alaska. In this report, Alaska statewide multipliers are used to estimate impacts for parks in Alaska.

Estimates for Katmai and Denali are based on recent studies (Fay and Christensen 2010; Stynes and Ackerman 2010). Both of these studies made adjustments to the number of park visits. Spending was based on a 2006 visitor survey at Katmai (Littlejohn and Hollenhorst 2008). Fay and Christensen estimated $48 million in spending by Katmai visitors within Alaska in 2006, of which $10.8 million was reported in the local park area. The 2006 Denali visitor survey did not include spending questions. Spending was therefore estimated using an engineering approach based on local room taxes, rail passengers, and other local data sources. This has the advantage of grounding the estimates in local economic data. Based on the study, the 2008 visitor spending estimate for Denali NP was increased from $43.8 million to $154 million (Stynes and Ackerman 2010). The revised Denali estimate includes $50 million in transportation spending (air, rail, bus, car rentals), most of which accrues to firms outside the local region, and also $17.7 million in tour revenues. Since virtually all tourism activity in the Denali area is associated with park visits, the impact estimates were validated against local employment and sales figures. These two studies illustrate some of the difficulties of estimating impacts for Alaska parks.

Similar studies at other Alaska parks would likely yield different estimates from those reported here, especially if spending beyond the local region were included. A visit to one or more national parks is an important part of the trip for most Alaska visitors. One could therefore argue to count a substantial portion of tourism spending in Alaska as related to national park visits. The U.S. Travel Association estimated tourist spending in Alaska at $2.1 billion in 2008 (USTA 2010). This is ten times what we have included as spending by park visitors in the local regions around Alaska national parks. Including spending in Alaska outside the local regions would significantly increase the estimates; however, deciding which spending to include would be somewhat subjective.

References

Fay, G., and N. Christensen. 2010. Katmai National Park and Preserve economic impact analysis and model documentation. Report to National Parks and Conservation Association and National Park Service.

Littlejohn, M. and S. Hollenhorst. 2008. Katmai National Park and Preserve visitor study, summer 2006. Visitor Service Project Report #182. University of Idaho Park Studies Unit, Moscow, Idaho.

Minnesota IMPLAN Group Inc. 2010. IMPLAN Pro Version 3.0, user's guide. Stillwater, Minnesota.

National Park Service (NPS). 2010. Statistical abstract, 2009. Natural Resource Report NPS/NRPC/NRR-2010-039. Natural Resource Program Center, Public Use Statistics Office, Denver, Colorado.

Stynes, D. J. 2008. Impacts of visitor spending on the local economy: Saint-Gaudens National Historic Site, 2004. Department of Community, Agriculture, Recreation, and Resource Studies, Michigan State University, East Lansing, Michigan.

———. 2009. National park visitor spending and payroll impacts, 2008. Report to National Park Service. Department of Community, Agriculture, Recreation and Resource Studies, Michigan State University, East Lansing, Michigan.

Stynes, D. J. and A. Ackerman. 2010. Impacts of visitor spending on the local economy: Denali National Park and Preserve, 2008. Department of Community, Agriculture, Recreation and Resource Studies, Michigan State University, East Lansing, Michigan.

Stynes, D. J., D. B. Propst, W. H. Chang, and Y. Sun. 2000. Estimating regional economic impacts of park visitor spending: Money Generation Model Version 2 (MGM2). Department of Park, Recreation and Tourism Resources, Michigan State University, East Lansing, Michigan.

Stynes, D. J. and Y. Sun. 2005. Economic impacts of Grand Canyon National Park visitor spending on the local economy, 2003. Department of Park, Recreation and Tourism Resources, Michigan State University, East Lansing, Michigan.

U.S. Travel Association (USTA). 2010. The power of travel, economic impact of travel and tourism. Available at http://www.poweroftravel.org/statistics/.

Appendices

Table A-1. Spending and Economic Impacts of National Park Visitors on Local Economies, CY 2009..18

Table A-2. Payroll Impacts of National Park Units on Local Economies, FY 2009..............27

Table A-3. Payroll Impacts of National Park Units on Local Economies, Administrative Units and Parks without Visit Counts, FY 2009......................................35

Table A-4. Impacts of NPS Visitor Spending and Payroll on Local Economies by State, 2009...38

Table A-5. Impacts of NPS Visitor Spending and Payroll on Local Economies by Region, 2009...40

Table A-6. Allocations to States for Multi-state Parks...41

Table A-1. Spending and Economic Impacts of National Park Visitors on Local Economies, CY 2009

Park Unit	Public Use Data		Visitor Spending 2009		Impacts of Non-Local Visitor Spending		
	2009 Recreation Visits	2009 Overnight Stays	All Visitors ($000's)	Non-Local Visitors ($000's)	Jobs	Labor Income ($000's)	Value Added ($000's)
Abraham Lincoln Birthplace NHP	221,111	0	7,448	6,937	115	3,131	5,247
Acadia NP	2,227,698	136,046	161,489	159,106	2,763	65,809	110,965
Adams NHP	253,656	0	15,867	14,779	217	8,312	13,858
Agate Fossil Beds NM	12,694	0	740	735	13	257	428
Alibates Flint Quarries NM	2,918	0	140	131	2	41	66
Allegheny Portage Railroad NHS	118,931	0	5,723	5,330	87	2,051	3,422
Amistad NRA	2,573,966	32,205	71,260	62,041	938	18,228	30,924
Andersonville NHS	136,267	0	4,590	4,275	72	1,642	2,765
Andrew Johnson NHS	63,296	0	3,046	2,837	46	1,199	2,026
Antietam NB	378,966	0	18,070	16,303	229	8,568	14,507
*Apostle Islands NL	170,202	27,589	18,203	17,833	301	6,190	10,222
Appomattox Court House NHP	185,443	0	8,923	8,311	129	3,054	5,219
*Arches NP	996,312	54,274	99,918	99,918	1,544	32,630	55,576
Arkansas Post NMEM	32,160	0	1,083	1,009	18	310	529
Arlington House, Robert E. Lee MEM	603,773	0	37,769	35,179	403	16,372	27,316
Assateague Island NS	2,129,658	112,681	139,828	132,995	1,981	54,536	93,670
Aztec Ruins NM	38,234	0	1,151	1,115	16	389	668
*Badlands NP	933,918	46,255	21,323	21,323	327	7,672	12,904
Bandelier NM	212,544	13,937	9,061	8,764	98	2,107	3,534
Bent's Old Fort NHS	28,131	0	948	883	13	264	446
Bering Land Bridge NPRES	1,054	1,986	316	316	3	112	199
Big Bend NP	363,905	170,616	15,391	14,736	219	4,746	8,374
Big Cypress NPRES	812,207	29,025	93,637	91,801	1,359	47,228	79,169
Big Hole NB	49,822	0	1,678	1,563	27	542	933
Big South Fork NRRA	686,747	69,420	26,794	23,434	324	7,063	11,985
Big Thicket NPRES	100,509	2,722	6,600	6,272	90	2,938	5,130
Bighorn Canyon NRA	205,293	14,253	5,773	5,058	79	1,934	3,326
Biscayne NP	437,745	8,317	27,368	27,038	342	11,802	20,213
Black Canyon of the Gunnison NP	171,451	14,524	7,861	7,482	106	2,416	4,192
Blue Ridge Parkway	15,936,316	149,616	315,552	288,542	4,046	83,761	141,357
Bluestone NSR	45,904	0	1,883	1,647	20	372	612
Booker T. Washington NM	21,216	0	1,021	951	15	378	640
Boston African American NHS	298,519	0	18,674	17,393	217	9,023	14,954
Boston NHP	2,155,026	0	73,268	70,865	901	37,822	63,084
Brown V. Board of Education NHS	19,228	0	925	862	15	408	693
Bryce Canyon NP	1,216,377	149,965	99,405	98,468	1,529	29,914	51,693
Buck Island Reef NM	47,341	3,920	3,103	2,953	45	926	1,580
Buffalo National River	1,522,586	112,493	44,793	39,493	541	12,871	22,134
Cabrillo NM	767,687	0	48,023	44,730	587	19,342	32,875
Canaveral NS	1,001,665	2,081	65,972	62,670	986	31,161	53,179

Table A-1. Spending and Economic Impacts of National Park Visitors on Local Economies, CY 2009 (continued)

Park Unit	Public Use Data		Visitor Spending 2009		Impacts of Non-Local Visitor Spending		
	2009 Recreation Visits	2009 Overnight Stays	All Visitors ($000's)	Non-Local Visitors ($000's)	Jobs	Labor Income ($000's)	Value Added ($000's)
Cane River Creole NHP	27,411	0	1,319	1,229	20	428	716
Canyon de Chelly NM	826,425	55,114	39,238	36,603	512	11,317	19,409
Canyonlands NP	436,241	90,033	33,625	33,297	460	11,371	19,785
Cape Cod NS	4,311,949	22,562	153,073	122,040	1,649	55,556	94,619
Cape Hatteras NS	2,282,543	86,765	108,482	103,105	1,551	38,547	66,529
Cape Krusenstern NM	1,810	1,775	543	543	6	188	327
Cape Lookout NS	601,954	36,813	41,696	39,774	642	13,386	22,782
Capitol Reef NP	617,208	35,489	34,290	34,102	604	11,275	19,473
*Capulin Volcano NM	50,935	0	1,339	1,315	17	329	567
Carl Sandburg Home NHS	83,550	0	4,020	3,745	56	1,378	2,318
Carlsbad Caverns NP	432,639	114	22,702	22,137	323	6,420	10,992
Casa Grande Ruins NM	76,350	0	2,134	2,003	21	470	761
Castillo de San Marcos NM	667,783	0	41,773	38,909	517	14,672	25,263
Castle Clinton NM	4,080,152	0	72,733	50,415	540	23,397	38,816
Catoctin Mountain Park	440,294	36,394	21,584	20,185	230	9,347	15,538
Cedar Breaks NM	492,353	910	16,591	15,455	247	5,660	9,650
Chaco Culture NHP	37,376	4,766	1,011	971	13	280	475
Chamizal NMEM	215,852	0	13,503	12,577	212	4,918	8,556
Channel Islands NP	348,745	55,663	29,569	28,145	365	13,337	22,268
Charles Pinckney NHS	43,447	0	2,091	1,947	30	811	1,401
Chattahoochee River NRA	2,830,655	0	80,596	54,183	662	23,437	39,570
*Chesapeake & Ohio Canal NHP	3,751,681	4,770	46,931	30,180	392	15,326	25,527
Chickamauga & Chattanooga NMP	992,448	1,951	47,777	44,506	693	20,134	34,235
Chickasaw NRA	1,238,484	72,332	15,831	12,297	164	3,236	5,529
Chiricahua NM	60,851	8,997	3,028	2,840	37	862	1,463
Christiansted NHS	114,743	0	3,865	3,600	54	1,112	1,891
City of Rocks NRES	96,649	0	6,367	6,048	84	1,974	3,323
Clara Barton NHS	10,986	0	687	640	7	298	497
*Colonial NHP	3,324,751	0	56,896	52,318	777	19,515	34,135
Colorado NM	400,266	16,586	19,439	18,143	257	6,282	10,675
Congaree NP	122,970	3,978	2,767	2,454	46	1,109	1,895
Coronado NMEM	106,409	0	3,584	3,338	47	1,249	2,124
Cowpens NB	224,394	0	10,798	10,057	171	4,330	7,403
*Crater Lake NP	446,516	80,053	32,862	31,880	512	12,034	20,410
*Craters of the Moon NM & PRES	194,046	14,150	5,735	5,676	80	1,685	2,890
Cumberland Gap NHP	883,663	16,415	42,681	39,790	637	12,746	21,449
Cumberland Island NS	77,588	17,087	5,019	4,791	75	2,264	3,862
Curecanti NRA	953,169	56,971	38,219	33,453	442	10,117	17,463
Cuyahoga Valley NP	2,589,288	2,293	54,286	39,127	571	16,438	27,618
*Dayton Aviation Heritage NHP	58,301	0	2,895	2,740	52	1,258	2,134
De Soto NMEM	246,608	0	15,427	14,369	238	7,419	12,587

Table A-1. Spending and Economic Impacts of National Park Visitors on Local Economies, CY 2009 (continued)

Park Unit	Public Use Data		Visitor Spending 2009		Impacts of Non-Local Visitor Spending		
	2009 Recreation Visits	2009 Overnight Stays	All Visitors ($000's)	Non-Local Visitors ($000's)	Jobs	Labor Income ($000's)	Value Added ($000's)
Death Valley NP	828,574	212,955	40,255	38,602	422	10,225	16,953
Delaware Water Gap NRA	5,213,030	109,764	108,578	94,196	1,144	33,491	59,337
*Denali NP & PRES	358,041	89,858	154,721	154,721	2,319	77,394	125,922
Devils Postpile NM	110,212	5,144	3,752	3,503	51	1,341	2,250
Devils Tower NM	391,023	13,860	13,278	12,390	196	4,586	7,835
Dinosaur NM	203,862	44,883	6,631	6,203	75	1,989	3,462
Dry Tortugas NP	52,011	13,003	4,390	4,194	48	1,649	2,860
Edgar Allan Poe NHS	17,463	0	1,092	1,017	15	541	907
*Effigy Mounds NM	78,177	0	4,374	4,193	77	1,335	2,247
*Eisenhower NHS	64,212	0	3,950	3,919	61	1,361	2,301
El Malpais NM	123,290	461	4,340	4,180	68	1,759	2,994
El Morro NM	48,245	3,123	1,611	1,544	21	425	739
Eleanor Roosevelt NHS	54,393	0	894	554	8	212	358
Eugene O'Neill NHS	3,783	0	237	220	3	118	200
*Everglades NP	900,882	33,249	162,343	157,552	2,361	83,059	139,886
Federal Hall NMEM	204,880	0	12,816	11,937	132	6,356	10,636
Fire Island NS	569,667	38,735	31,519	27,657	345	13,478	22,747
First Ladies NHS	10,466	0	655	610	10	223	374
Flight 93 NMEM	149,668	0	7,202	6,708	105	2,442	4,079
Florissant Fossil Beds NM	64,251	0	3,092	2,880	38	1,091	1,863
Ford's Theatre NHS	658,271	0	20,773	19,046	222	9,228	15,561
Fort Bowie NHS	9,641	0	464	432	6	135	228
Fort Caroline NMEM	288,606	0	18,054	16,816	262	7,955	13,535
Fort Davis NHS	50,968	0	1,717	1,599	23	475	823
Fort Donelson NB	203,456	205	6,855	6,385	100	2,046	3,469
Fort Frederica NM	296,117	0	14,249	13,272	191	5,012	8,515
Fort Laramie NHS	56,923	0	1,917	1,786	28	607	1,049
*Fort Larned NHS	27,443	0	1,430	1,416	25	496	830
Fort Matanzas NM	793,253	0	49,622	46,219	614	17,428	30,009
Fort McHenry NM & HS	605,870	0	37,900	35,301	452	14,003	23,593
Fort Necessity NB	197,271	710	6,043	5,310	77	1,680	2,819
Fort Point NHS	1,385,134	0	86,647	80,706	873	39,526	66,804
Fort Pulaski NM	435,661	10	20,964	19,526	295	8,179	14,012
Fort Raleigh NHS	338,212	0	11,392	10,611	170	4,226	7,317
Fort Scott NHS	28,544	0	961	896	15	278	466
Fort Smith NHS	63,540	0	3,057	2,848	51	1,061	1,778
*Fort Stanwix NM	93,170	0	3,294	3,152	46	1,161	1,922
Fort Sumter NM	785,604	5	17,188	15,284	208	5,379	9,139
Fort Union NM	11,070	0	237	227	3	65	109
Fort Union Trading Post NHS	15,141	0	989	959	15	300	512
Fort Vancouver NHS	1,017,326	0	48,953	45,596	773	23,830	40,319
Fort Washington Park	339,370	0	10,710	9,819	115	4,758	8,022
Fossil Butte NM	18,693	0	630	586	9	188	324

Table A-1. Spending and Economic Impacts of National Park Visitors on Local Economies, CY 2009 (continued)

Park Unit	Public Use Data		Visitor Spending 2009		Impacts of Non-Local Visitor Spending		
	2009 Recreation Visits	2009 Overnight Stays	All Visitors ($000's)	Non-Local Visitors ($000's)	Jobs	Labor Income ($000's)	Value Added ($000's)
Franklin Delano Roosevelt Memorial	2,591,241	0	81,773	74,973	875	36,326	61,254
Frederick Douglass NHS	43,483	0	1,372	1,258	15	610	1,028
Frederick Law Olmsted NHS	5,007	0	313	292	4	151	251
Fredericksburg & Spotsylvania NMP	906,175	0	43,604	40,614	569	14,223	24,670
Friendship Hill NHS	31,454	0	1,968	1,833	28	632	1,074
Gates of the Arctic NP & PRES	9,975	4,638	2,993	2,993	32	1,043	1,821
Gateway NRA	9,010,522	8,933	157,979	64,208	707	33,515	56,166
Gauley River NRA	113,185	4,738	4,515	3,944	56	1,436	2,415
General Grant NMEM	100,874	0	6,310	5,877	65	3,129	5,237
George Rogers Clark NHP	103,284	0	4,970	4,629	77	1,423	2,402
*George Washington Birthplace NM	113,083	0	2,501	1,579	24	459	792
George Washington Carver NM	38,899	0	1,872	1,743	29	599	996
George Washington MEM PKWY	6,938,309	0	28,526	4,156	46	1,762	2,936
*Gettysburg NMP	1,013,002	23,993	61,207	60,729	951	21,082	35,648
Gila Cliff Dwellings NM	43,016	0	1,092	1,052	15	271	465
Glacier Bay NP & PRES	438,361	16,635	3,217	3,217	41	1,267	2,190
Glacier NP	2,031,348	379,619	97,371	93,711	1,432	34,629	60,975
Glen Canyon NRA	1,960,345	1,580,992	152,205	152,205	1,790	47,106	77,666
Golden Gate NRA	15,036,372	78,110	269,028	113,337	1,479	59,191	100,282
*Golden Spike NHS	45,334	0	2,075	2,027	34	727	1,217
Governors Island NM	325,840	0	27,906	26,508	295	14,371	24,074
*Grand Canyon NP	4,348,068	1,269,839	405,226	405,226	5,521	139,112	233,404
Grand Portage NM	76,025	60	8,190	8,149	130	2,762	4,781
*Grand Teton NP	2,580,081	552,358	397,322	393,913	5,928	144,997	250,741
Grant-Kohrs Ranch NHS	20,099	0	677	631	11	253	438
Great Basin NP	84,974	29,988	3,831	3,671	49	979	1,672
Great Sand Dunes NP & PRES	289,955	51,292	10,114	9,497	137	2,979	5,082
Great Smoky Mountains NP	9,491,437	400,832	799,608	774,996	11,112	282,668	487,083
Greenbelt Park	188,043	23,176	12,097	11,334	129	5,235	8,689
Guadalupe Mountains NP	198,882	19,076	13,014	12,390	189	3,520	6,047
Guilford Courthouse NMP	290,368	9	13,972	13,014	224	5,881	9,830
Gulf Islands NS	4,132,674	28,601	109,611	62,907	883	22,385	38,484
Hagerman Fossil Beds NM	27,263	0	799	698	11	242	413
Haleakala NP	1,109,104	17,231	72,989	69,359	813	30,159	51,784
Hamilton Grange NMEM	150	0	9	9	0	5	8
Hampton NHS	39,334	0	2,461	2,292	29	909	1,532
Harpers Ferry NHP	275,044	0	9,977	9,123	129	3,838	6,425
Harry S Truman NHS	28,384	0	1,776	1,654	25	887	1,542
Hawaii Volcanoes NP	1,233,105	114,170	82,654	78,783	1,076	35,599	61,322
Herbert Hoover NHS	162,886	0	7,838	7,300	121	2,857	4,890

Table A-1. Spending and Economic Impacts of National Park Visitors on Local Economies, CY 2009 (continued)

Park Unit	Public Use Data		Visitor Spending 2009		Impacts of Non-Local Visitor Spending		
	2009 Recreation Visits	2009 Overnight Stays	All Visitors ($000's)	Non-Local Visitors ($000's)	Jobs	Labor Income ($000's)	Value Added ($000's)
Home of Franklin D. Roosevelt NHS	123,033	0	2,416	2,128	30	835	1,409
*Homestead National Monument of America	71,301	0	2,078	1,946	35	708	1,171
Hopewell Culture NHP	34,179	0	1,151	1,072	17	347	581
Hopewell Furnace NHS	53,186	0	2,559	2,384	37	1,058	1,777
Horseshoe Bend NMP	72,232	0	3,476	3,237	52	1,054	1,790
Hot Springs NP	1,284,707	9,615	84,596	80,373	1,334	27,397	46,761
Hovenweep NM	27,855	1,628	1,358	1,269	18	435	757
Hubbell Trading Post NHS	99,267	0	4,777	4,449	61	1,223	2,184
Independence NHP	3,967,694	0	148,929	133,374	1,889	67,773	113,569
Indiana Dunes NL	1,944,568	28,117	54,878	38,438	542	12,681	21,284
Isle Royale NP	14,653	42,864	1,798	1,798	26	546	945
*James A. Garfield NHS	17,100	0	510	466	7	211	357
Jean Lafitte NHP & PRES	335,075	0	16,124	15,018	210	7,083	12,086
Jefferson National Expansion Memorial	2,360,109	0	91,834	80,868	1,182	33,015	54,952
Jewel Cave NM	129,595	0	6,236	5,808	98	2,236	3,813
Jimmy Carter NHS	69,972	0	2,357	2,195	36	678	1,139
John D Rockefeller Jr. MEM PKWY	1,139,923	28,489	5,981	5,501	72	1,780	3,024
*John Day Fossil Beds NM	130,925	275	5,648	5,563	74	1,480	2,574
John F. Kennedy NHS	16,333	0	1,022	952	12	494	818
John Muir NHS	34,516	0	2,159	2,011	28	907	1,535
Johnstown Flood NMEM	114,350	0	6,272	5,804	104	2,425	4,077
*Joshua Tree NP	1,304,471	266,226	32,525	28,395	334	9,688	16,055
Kalaupapa NHP	30,654	0	1,475	1,374	16	586	1,003
Kaloko-Honokohau NHP	166,380	0	8,006	7,457	101	3,323	5,699
*Katmai NP & PRES/Aniakchak NM & PRES	43,035	4,744	9,601	9,488	93	2,386	3,920
Kenai Fjords NP	218,358	2,099	6,706	6,610	89	2,734	4,777
Kennesaw Mountain NBP	1,372,228	0	41,049	35,669	477	16,294	27,591
*Kings Mountain NMP	277,576	87	9,220	8,251	135	2,871	4,943
Klondike Gold Rush NHP Alaska	880,512	5,006	21,897	21,633	266	8,364	14,481
Klondike Gold Rush NHP Seattle	54,219	0	3,392	3,159	46	1,638	2,783
Knife River Indian Villages NHS	29,390	0	990	922	17	371	624
Kobuk Valley NP	1,879	1,966	564	564	6	196	342
Korean War Veterans Memorial	3,117,046	0	98,366	90,187	1,053	43,697	73,683
Lake Chelan NRA	34,554	16,049	1,400	1,304	18	658	1,124
Lake Clark NP & PRES	9,711	3,321	2,913	2,913	31	1,008	1,752
Lake Mead NRA	7,668,689	984,797	265,672	225,958	2,394	79,416	130,221
Lake Meredith NRA	1,080,644	37,606	43,024	37,554	492	11,127	17,920
Lake Roosevelt NRA	1,382,663	140,047	39,623	34,884	498	11,754	19,809

Table A-1. Spending and Economic Impacts of National Park Visitors on Local Economies, CY 2009 (continued)

Park Unit	Public Use Data		Visitor Spending 2009		Impacts of Non-Local Visitor Spending		
	2009 Recreation Visits	2009 Overnight Stays	All Visitors ($000's)	Non-Local Visitors ($000's)	Jobs	Labor Income ($000's)	Value Added ($000's)
Lassen Volcanic NP	365,639	98,931	14,678	13,400	185	4,912	8,170
Lava Beds NM	129,639	10,154	4,236	4,048	55	1,251	2,115
LBJ Memorial Grove on the Potomac	333,368	0	20,854	19,424	223	9,040	15,082
Lewis & Clark NHP	225,846	0	10,868	10,122	151	3,126	5,316
Lincoln Boyhood NMEM	182,172	0	8,766	8,165	135	2,649	4,515
Lincoln Home NHS	464,074	0	23,591	23,166	373	9,669	16,020
Lincoln Memorial	5,255,570	0	165,853	152,062	1,775	73,676	124,235
Little Bighorn Battlefield NM	302,811	0	10,200	9,500	158	3,823	6,588
Little River Canyon NPRES	189,251	0	8,727	8,290	142	2,828	4,799
Little Rock Central High School NHS	60,103	0	2,892	2,694	44	1,235	2,067
Longfellow NHS	39,065	0	1,880	1,751	23	811	1,357
Lowell NHP	565,960	0	35,404	32,976	432	15,280	25,564
Lyndon B. Johnson NHP	98,218	0	6,144	5,723	77	2,290	3,928
Maggie L Walker NHS	9,853	0	224	120	2	55	94
Mammoth Cave NP	503,856	88,876	32,303	30,577	525	11,514	19,202
Manassas NBP	578,383	0	7,442	7,120	82	2,720	4,605
*Manzanar NHS	89,190	0	8,496	8,435	100	2,531	4,368
Marsh-Billings-Rockefeller NHP	31,129	0	1,498	1,395	20	560	955
Martin Luther King, Jr. NHS	650,343	0	40,682	37,893	495	18,128	30,786
Martin Van Buren NHS	23,216	0	437	382	5	130	211
Mary McLeod Bethune Council House NHS	21,811	0	688	631	7	306	516
Mesa Verde NP	550,377	92,438	39,224	37,573	529	13,053	22,258
Minute Man NHP	1,096,024	0	68,562	63,860	836	29,590	49,506
*Minuteman Missile NHS	36,777	0	2,352	2,352	40	920	1,564
Missouri National Recreational River	186,313	0	8,592	8,162	171	2,352	3,986
Mojave NPRES	528,865	2,180	10,780	9,402	112	3,875	6,356
*Monocacy NB	34,553	0	2,418	2,247	27	1,048	1,796
Montezuma Castle NM	601,465	0	28,942	26,957	411	13,337	22,862
Moores Creek NB	68,864	481	2,313	2,154	37	827	1,442
Morristown NHP	298,060	0	14,342	13,359	171	6,245	10,554
*Mount Rainier NP	1,151,654	169,439	32,908	31,373	431	11,972	19,958
Mount Rushmore NMEM	2,260,192	0	71,635	67,420	1,039	23,780	40,273
Muir Woods NM	779,880	0	48,785	45,440	571	23,645	40,133
Natchez NHP	218,126	0	10,496	9,776	136	2,795	4,900
Natchez Trace PKWY	5,934,363	19,071	84,820	30,714	409	8,450	14,150
National Capital Parks-Central	3,678,876	0	116,096	106,443	1,242	51,573	86,964
National Capital Parks-East	1,272,212	0	40,148	36,809	430	17,835	30,074
Natural Bridges NM	92,023	6,406	4,499	4,205	58	1,189	2,084
Navajo NM	77,901	2,723	3,772	3,519	46	1,140	1,938
New Bedford Whaling NHP	279,803	0	17,503	16,303	241	7,370	12,463

Table A-1. Spending and Economic Impacts of National Park Visitors on Local Economies, CY 2009 (continued)

Park Unit	Public Use Data		Visitor Spending 2009		Impacts of Non-Local Visitor Spending		
	2009 Recreation Visits	2009 Overnight Stays	All Visitors ($000's)	Non-Local Visitors ($000's)	Jobs	Labor Income ($000's)	Value Added ($000's)
New Orleans Jazz NHP	80,828	0	3,889	3,623	51	1,709	2,915
*New River Gorge NR	1,144,318	10,996	43,790	41,253	491	8,931	14,809
Nez Perce NHP	176,238	0	5,936	5,529	94	1,939	3,269
Nicodemus NHS	2,978	0	129	126	2	28	46
Ninety Six NHS	50,689	0	2,439	2,272	37	726	1,231
Niobrara NSR	68,058	0	3,139	2,981	62	859	1,456
Noatak NPRES	2,474	2,221	742	742	8	259	452
North Cascades NP	26,972	14,646	1,660	1,590	22	803	1,368
Obed Wild and Scenic River	212,933	1,644	8,755	7,663	116	2,590	4,304
Ocmulgee NM	110,819	0	5,333	4,967	86	2,005	3,399
*Olympic NP	3,276,459	342,573	113,699	104,398	1,552	36,338	61,751
Oregon Caves NM	88,496	6,322	4,090	3,809	62	1,461	2,450
Organ Pipe Cactus NM	330,064	19,382	16,082	15,022	231	7,460	12,789
Ozark National Scenic Riverways	1,308,718	139,239	55,445	49,046	696	15,931	27,883
Padre Island NS	642,163	69,701	41,965	39,961	641	16,193	27,266
Palo Alto Battlefield NHP	41,599	0	1,401	1,305	22	499	841
Pea Ridge NMP	68,746	0	3,308	3,081	55	947	1,617
Pecos NHP	34,522	0	721	698	11	293	497
Pennsylvania Avenue NHS	256,874	0	8,106	7,432	87	3,601	6,072
*Perry's Victory and International Peace MEM	154,457	3,058	11,605	11,605	201	4,726	7,961
Petersburg NB	162,722	0	7,830	7,293	122	2,923	5,069
Petrified Forest NP	631,613	5,734	41,608	39,524	593	12,739	21,925
Petroglyph NM	118,688	0	4,789	3,904	67	1,797	3,066
*Pictured Rocks NL	448,215	28,417	18,199	17,894	300	4,158	7,139
Pinnacles NM	171,112	9,524	3,208	2,687	31	1,087	1,864
Pipe Spring NM	49,433	0	2,379	2,216	31	773	1,310
Pipestone NM	69,539	0	2,889	2,805	46	1,143	1,963
Piscataway Park	234,186	0	7,390	6,776	79	3,283	5,536
Point Reyes NS	2,170,646	41,230	85,751	78,206	966	39,334	66,016
President's Park	1,475,182	0	46,553	42,682	498	20,680	34,872
Prince William Forest Park	368,365	57,226	19,330	14,657	165	6,707	10,849
Pu'uhonua o Honaunau NHP	397,665	0	19,135	17,823	242	7,942	13,622
Puukohola Heiau NHS	99,042	0	4,766	4,439	60	1,978	3,393
Rainbow Bridge NM	113,460	0	5,460	5,085	64	1,611	2,719
Redwood NP	444,426	14,561	21,644	19,605	272	6,234	10,418
Richmond NBP	134,634	0	9,235	8,344	135	3,903	6,656
Rio Grande Wild and Scenic River	947	4,661	92	90	1	24	42
Rock Creek Park	2,076,500	0	65,529	60,080	701	29,110	49,086
Rocky Mountain NP	2,822,325	170,871	229,032	221,896	3,316	89,975	155,157
Roger Williams NMEM	50,397	0	3,153	2,936	46	1,496	2,487
Ross Lake NRA	288,458	63,811	8,807	7,875	107	3,876	6,592

Table A-1. Spending and Economic Impacts of National Park Visitors on Local Economies, CY 2009 (continued)

Park Unit	Public Use Data		Visitor Spending 2009		Impacts of Non-Local Visitor Spending		
	2009 Recreation Visits	2009 Overnight Stays	All Visitors ($000's)	Non-Local Visitors ($000's)	Jobs	Labor Income ($000's)	Value Added ($000's)
Russell Cave NM	24,087	0	1,159	1,080	17	337	569
Sagamore Hill NHS	53,800	0	3,365	3,135	39	1,541	2,600
Saguaro NP	665,234	1,599	21,608	15,030	203	5,364	9,075
Saint Croix NSR	564,326	88,928	16,328	14,423	222	5,904	9,942
Saint Paul's Church NHS	14,432	0	903	841	9	448	749
*Saint-Gaudens NHS	34,558	0	1,277	1,176	19	507	867
Salem Maritime NHS	723,088	0	45,233	42,131	549	17,133	28,763
Salinas Pueblo Missions NM	37,848	0	936	902	14	386	657
San Antonio Missions NHP	1,567,667	0	58,843	52,697	784	23,147	39,192
San Francisco Maritime NHP	4,152,497	11,208	82,915	61,353	620	27,472	46,037
San Juan Island NHP	274,642	0	17,180	16,002	207	5,558	9,433
San Juan NHS	1,069,673	0	51,472	47,942	683	16,485	29,297
Santa Monica Mountains NRA	501,573	144	19,545	13,020	171	6,213	10,378
Saratoga NHP	89,366	0	3,010	2,804	36	979	1,639
Saugus Iron Works NHS	10,529	0	659	613	8	314	521
Scotts Bluff NM	121,391	0	3,795	3,100	57	1,091	1,793
*Sequoia NP/ Kings Canyon NP[a]	1,279,341	259,107	88,967[a]	81,613	1,209	32,694	55,342
Shenandoah NP	1,120,981	293,200	63,174	56,080	797	21,246	37,441
Shiloh NMP	404,134	0	13,613	12,679	206	4,315	7,407
Sitka NHP	246,866	0	4,709	4,652	57	1,798	3,112
*Sleeping Bear Dunes NL	1,165,836	112,221	107,165	104,441	1,803	45,168	78,134
Springfield Armory NHS	17,779	0	1,112	1,036	15	506	847
Statue of Liberty NM	3,829,483	0	159,908	144,144	1,582	74,022	123,900
Steamtown NHS	65,144	0	2,194	2,044	34	902	1,495
Stones River NB	189,952	0	9,140	8,514	128	4,331	7,275
Sunset Crater Volcano NM	187,397	0	9,017	8,399	109	2,814	4,735
Tallgrass Prairie NPRES	23,713	0	1,094	1,039	17	296	500
Thaddeus Kosciuszko NMEM	3,357	0	210	196	3	104	174
Theodore Roosevelt Birthplace NHS	14,390	0	900	838	9	446	747
Theodore Roosevelt Inaugural NHS	11,735	0	734	684	11	307	507
Theodore Roosevelt Island Park	141,559	0	8,855	8,248	95	3,839	6,404
Theodore Roosevelt NP	586,928	26,814	26,987	25,664	455	8,790	14,671
Thomas Edison NHP	27,061	0	1,693	1,577	20	764	1,284
Thomas Jefferson Memorial	2,337,868	0	73,777	67,643	789	32,774	55,264
Thomas Stone NHS	6,268	0	392	365	5	127	218
Timpanogos Cave NM	138,571	0	8,668	8,074	137	3,881	6,555
Timucuan Ecological & Historic PRES	1,195,171	0	58,878	46,062	703	21,384	36,354
Tonto NM	60,534	0	2,913	2,713	42	1,368	2,349
Tumacacori NHP	40,637	0	1,369	1,275	18	477	811
Tuskegee Airmen NHS	58,417	0	2,811	2,618	41	804	1,364

Table A-1. Spending and Economic Impacts of National Park Visitors on Local Economies, CY 2009 (continued)

Park Unit	Public Use Data		Visitor Spending 2009		Impacts of Non-Local Visitor Spending		
	2009 Recreation Visits	2009 Overnight Stays	All Visitors ($000's)	Non-Local Visitors ($000's)	Jobs	Labor Income ($000's)	Value Added ($000's)
Tuskegee Institute NHS	31,360	0	1,509	1,406	22	432	732
Tuzigoot NM	106,250	0	5,113	4,762	73	2,356	4,039
Ulysses S. Grant NHS	40,703	0	2,546	2,372	35	1,001	1,668
Upper Delaware SRR	258,311	0	7,419	6,488	87	2,164	3,661
USS Arizona Memorial	1,276,868	0	47,928	42,922	622	21,473	35,988
*Valley Forge NHP	1,449,228	1,500	50,699	36,396	558	21,170	35,725
Vanderbilt Mansion NHS	380,460	0	5,297	3,094	41	1,136	1,905
Vicksburg NMP	584,105	0	28,107	26,179	403	10,239	17,206
Vietnam Veterans Memorial	4,437,771	0	140,045	128,400	1,499	62,212	104,903
*Virgin Islands NP	415,847	102,750	50,019	50,019	867	19,612	33,760
Voyageurs NP	222,429	48,971	10,285	9,825	166	3,581	6,013
Walnut Canyon NM	128,299	0	6,174	5,750	75	1,927	3,242
War in the Pacific NHP	271,608	0	9,149	8,521	98	3,966	6,617
Washington Monument	676,002	0	21,333	19,559	228	9,477	15,980
Washita Battlefield NHS	10,527	0	397	373	6	117	199
Weir Farm NHS	19,386	0	1,213	1,130	13	538	909
Whiskeytown-Shasta-Trinity NRA	853,812	49,624	34,180	29,906	432	11,067	18,334
White House	616,890	0	19,468	17,849	208	8,648	14,583
White Sands NM	471,167	1,751	15,970	15,666	243	4,678	8,076
Whitman Mission NHS	52,605	0	1,772	1,650	25	583	989
William Howard Taft NHS	18,802	0	1,176	1,096	17	519	866
Wilson's Creek NB	156,230	0	7,518	7,002	128	3,042	5,070
Wind Cave NP	587,868	2,103	38,719	36,783	525	14,213	24,109
Wolf Trap NP for the Performing Arts	466,752	0	29,198	27,196	312	12,657	21,116
*Women's Rights NHP	20,620	0	1,284	1,284	19	468	789
World War II Memorial	4,118,528	0	129,970	119,163	1,391	57,736	97,357
Wrangell-St Elias NP & PRES	59,966	0	2,551	2,551	30	973	1,757
Wright Brothers NMEM	476,291	0	16,043	14,943	240	5,951	10,304
Wupatki NM	233,284	0	11,225	10,456	136	3,503	5,895
*Yellowstone NP	3,295,187	1,275,647	296,989	296,989	4,369	114,135	197,993
*Yosemite NP	3,737,472	1,700,869	352,223	348,071	4,495	122,993	211,376
Yukon-Charley Rivers NPRES	6,432	15,562	5,281	5,281	58	1,880	3,339
*Zion NP	2,735,402	306,593	123,710	122,609	2,198	51,144	85,516

[a] Sequoia and Kings Canyon national parks are combined for the economic analysis. Recreation visits for the two parks are reduced to reflect double counting between the two parks.

* For these parks, results are based on a visitor survey at the designated park. For other parks, visitor characteristics and spending averages are adapted from national averages for each park type, adjusted for surrounding populations and spending opportunities.

Notes: Non-local visitors live outside a roughly 60-mile radius of the park. Jobs include part-time and full-time jobs with seasonal jobs adjusted to an annual basis. Impacts include direct and secondary effects of visitor spending on the local economy. Labor income covers wages and salaries, payroll benefits, and incomes of sole proprietors in the local region. Value added includes labor income, profits and rents, and indirect business taxes.

Table A-2. Payroll Impacts of National Park Units on Local Economies, FY 2009

	Park Payroll			Impacts of Park Payroll		
Park Unit	Salary	Payroll Benefits	NPS Jobs	Total Jobs	Labor Income ($000's)	Value Added ($000's)
Abraham Lincoln Birthplace NHP	878,507	190,036	22	28	1,272	1,640
Acadia NP	6,677,550	1,677,932	150	193	9,713	12,138
Adams NHP	1,434,458	292,844	30	39	2,210	3,053
Agate Fossil Beds NM	338,375	80,622	10	12	474	572
Allegheny Portage Railroad NHS	1,350,436	406,372	27	35	2,021	2,511
Amistad NRA	2,064,776	606,945	42	50	2,880	3,309
Andersonville NHS	994,556	246,788	21	26	1,407	1,720
Andrew Johnson NHS	508,129	111,247	11	15	736	949
Antietam NB	2,905,658	763,116	61	77	4,426	5,805
Apostle Islands NL	2,318,735	665,407	47	58	3,293	3,879
Appomattox Court House NHP	1,033,645	283,679	24	29	1,477	1,796
Arches NP	1,011,889	275,600	25	28	1,382	1,581
Arkansas Post NMEM	464,236	119,473	12	14	643	763
Arlington House, Robert E. Lee MEM	769,627	210,436	21	24	1,117	1,369
Assateague Island NS	3,560,847	890,866	85	107	5,225	6,692
Aztec Ruins NM	1,043,571	265,532	24	30	1,486	1,829
Badlands NP	3,474,787	938,180	80	98	5,046	6,190
Bandelier NM	3,533,231	1,073,088	92	92	4,622	4,666
Bent's Old Fort NHS	797,597	188,860	21	23	1,059	1,202
Bering Land Bridge NPRES	175,078	35,999	2	3	248	318
Big Bend NP	5,220,692	1,537,186	131	148	7,206	8,213
Big Cypress NPRES	4,738,644	1,383,969	89	118	7,277	9,386
Big South Fork NRRA	3,037,337	849,594	65	76	4,225	4,929
Big Thicket NPRES	2,112,217	597,271	50	60	3,138	3,960
Bighorn Canyon NRA	2,501,171	684,423	48	63	3,690	4,635
Biscayne NP	2,669,134	756,603	50	69	4,179	5,567
Black Canyon of the Gunnison NP	1,108,886	279,483	27	31	1,491	1,710
Blue Ridge Parkway	10,999,619	3,170,041	238	272	15,131	17,126
Bluestone NSR	54,720	18,965	1	1	74	74
Booker T. Washington NM	615,243	190,304	12	16	920	1,138
Boston African American NHS	447,055	88,198	14	17	652	854
Boston NHP	5,772,559	1,553,922	100	126	8,830	11,448
Brown V. Board of Education NHS	728,863	226,284	14	19	1,142	1,486
Bryce Canyon NP	3,230,921	884,748	89	99	4,365	4,908
Buck Island Reef NM	269,476	66,931	6	7	360	409
Buffalo National River	5,047,085	1,408,258	142	164	7,076	8,353
Cabrillo NM	1,200,789	310,235	27	33	1,751	2,203
Canaveral NS	2,481,265	648,854	54	72	3,820	5,097
Cane River Creole NHP	610,404	166,544	15	18	864	1,028
Canyon de Chelly NM	1,520,607	355,908	37	41	2,003	2,278

Table A-2. Payroll Impacts of National Park Units on Local Economies, FY 2009 (continued)

Park Unit	Park Payroll			Impacts of Park Payroll		
	Salary	Payroll Benefits	NPS Jobs	Total Jobs	Labor Income ($000's)	Value Added ($000's)
Canyonlands NP	5,289,500	1,429,949	131	149	7,266	8,444
Cape Cod NS	6,321,862	1,565,911	130	165	9,320	12,039
Cape Hatteras NS	5,631,861	1,465,968	134	168	8,201	10,409
Cape Lookout NS	1,834,345	386,336	44	52	2,413	2,804
Capitol Reef NP	1,762,492	487,643	38	47	2,448	2,859
Capulin Volcano NM	487,733	134,462	12	13	651	710
Carl Sandburg Home NHS	806,968	184,783	21	25	1,119	1,356
Carlsbad Caverns NP	4,132,049	1,082,310	97	110	5,617	6,436
Casa Grande Ruins NM	703,545	199,565	16	16	905	910
Castillo de San Marcos NM	1,899,676	539,524	42	49	2,698	3,238
Castle Clinton NM	243,804	69,132	5	6	371	475
Catoctin Mountain Park	2,282,936	586,874	48	56	3,277	4,025
Cedar Breaks NM	535,223	118,365	13	17	753	940
Chaco Culture NHP	1,458,899	356,749	30	34	1,953	2,222
Chamizal NMEM	1,306,051	372,181	32	39	1,891	2,312
Channel Islands NP	4,475,875	1,200,513	82	102	6,615	8,313
Charles Pinckney NHS	328,167	95,067	6	9	492	626
Chattahoochee River NRA	2,071,693	535,329	40	49	3,004	3,738
Chesapeake & Ohio Canal NHP	6,843,745	1,835,516	140	164	9,899	12,142
Chickamauga & Chattanooga NMP	2,147,150	560,287	45	59	3,218	4,170
Chickasaw NRA	2,832,709	821,610	73	86	4,038	4,800
Chiricahua NM	1,034,874	272,846	21	24	1,388	1,560
Christiansted NHS	630,107	150,717	13	15	836	950
City of Rocks NRES	41,325	10,599	2	2	56	64
Clara Barton NHS	359,093	108,670	10	11	532	649
Colonial NHP	4,229,472	1,246,335	81	100	6,032	7,291
Colorado NM	1,366,327	307,727	36	42	1,866	2,236
Congaree NP	978,501	274,648	24	30	1,475	1,885
Coronado NMEM	850,848	292,771	17	21	1,281	1,542
Cowpens NB	454,647	115,518	14	17	673	864
Crater Lake NP	4,285,783	1,065,099	97	118	6,017	7,244
Craters of the Moon NM&PRES	1,077,175	308,595	22	24	1,459	1,615
Cumberland Gap NHP	2,414,610	748,052	57	67	3,448	4,026
Cumberland Island NS	1,442,751	474,678	28	37	2,246	2,853
Curecanti NRA	2,531,819	642,097	54	62	3,408	3,909
Cuyahoga Valley NP	8,344,998	2,192,501	181	223	12,253	15,366
Dayton Aviation Heritage NHP	1,223,244	294,365	24	32	1,786	2,274
De Soto NMEM	437,547	118,858	11	14	692	941
Death Valley NP	6,381,352	1,681,585	142	142	8,088	8,140
Delaware Water Gap NRA	7,204,207	1,781,616	124	157	10,372	12,820

Table A-2. Payroll Impacts of National Park Units on Local Economies, FY 2009 (continued)

Park Unit	Park Payroll			Impacts of Park Payroll		
	Salary	Payroll Benefits	NPS Jobs	Total Jobs	Labor Income ($000's)	Value Added ($000's)
Denali NP & PRES	11,072,456	2,285,804	221	224	13,454	13,614
Devils Postpile NM	417,004	89,840	11	13	576	705
Devils Tower NM	891,877	218,685	21	25	1,253	1,524
Dinosaur NM	2,233,006	586,410	51	57	3,035	3,500
Dry Tortugas NP	779,984	222,950	15	18	1,120	1,371
Edgar Allan Poe NHS	271,729	86,518	5	6	441	588
Effigy Mounds NM	965,307	194,337	28	33	1,292	1,549
Eisenhower NHS	804,362	237,742	15	18	1,137	1,330
El Malpais NM	1,179,132	340,545	28	37	1,816	2,364
El Morro NM	583,114	149,967	15	16	786	903
Eleanor Roosevelt NHS	287,878	54,411	9	10	394	493
Eugene O'Neill NHS	325,732	83,652	8	9	497	655
Everglades NP	17,297,688	4,813,052	327	431	26,324	34,022
Federal Hall NMEM	312,103	57,676	12	13	444	578
Fire Island NS	3,438,656	751,172	66	82	4,988	6,444
Florissant Fossil Beds NM	718,270	195,775	18	21	1,027	1,248
Ford's Theatre NHS	0	0	4	4	0	0
Fort Bowie NHS	310,178	75,623	7	8	410	461
Fort Caroline NMEM	1,551,451	418,092	36	46	2,326	2,984
Fort Davis NHS	887,036	223,257	21	23	1,178	1,336
Fort Donelson NB	799,740	238,010	20	22	1,118	1,283
Fort Frederica NM	536,375	168,856	11	14	792	957
Fort Laramie NHS	1,185,542	305,932	28	33	1,649	1,965
Fort Larned NHS	732,621	218,788	17	20	1,063	1,269
Fort Matanzas NM	79,247	35,523	1	1	126	148
Fort McHenry NM & HS	1,400,734	339,726	31	36	1,953	2,358
Fort Necessity NB	972,988	298,331	18	23	1,425	1,721
Fort Point NHS	487,698	111,023	10	11	699	886
Fort Pulaski NM	897,561	201,942	26	31	1,281	1,624
Fort Raleigh NHS	216,042	55,899	6	7	314	399
Fort Scott NHS	915,968	211,817	20	24	1,230	1,443
Fort Smith NHS	611,398	166,618	13	17	876	1,059
Fort Stanwix NM	819,222	244,581	20	23	1,188	1,412
Fort Sumter NM	1,290,333	317,255	29	37	1,880	2,405
Fort Union NM	737,642	168,508	23	26	997	1,179
Fort Union Trading Post NHS	553,617	118,692	13	15	740	874
Fort Vancouver NHS	1,464,174	362,197	33	44	2,260	3,044
Fossil Butte NM	480,586	123,451	10	13	658	771
Frederick Douglass NHS	375,829	64,022	12	13	507	630
Frederick Law Olmsted NHS	1,166,948	308,432	20	26	1,779	2,309

Table A-2. Payroll Impacts of National Park Units on Local Economies, FY 2009 (continued)

Park Unit	Park Payroll			Impacts of Park Payroll		
	Salary	Payroll Benefits	NPS Jobs	Total Jobs	Labor Income ($000's)	Value Added ($000's)
Fredericksburg & Spotsylvania NMP	2,835,463	763,431	53	63	3,940	4,687
Friendship Hill NHS	409,181	141,293	9	11	615	739
Gates of the Arctic NP & PRES	1,489,835	311,788	37	46	2,115	2,712
Gateway NRA	18,877,891	4,268,553	369	442	27,644	35,711
Gauley River NRA	414,723	174,912	10	12	659	786
General Grant NMEM	232,872	69,316	6	6	358	457
George Rogers Clark NHP	634,530	176,135	14	16	874	1,005
George Washington Birthplace NM	1,200,388	319,841	29	32	1,620	1,861
George Washington Carver NM	616,870	154,103	15	18	861	1,031
George Washington MEM PKWY	5,875,697	1,619,396	123	143	8,542	10,468
Gettysburg NMP	4,971,287	1,166,555	84	103	6,725	7,915
Gila Cliff Dwellings NM	148,745	27,759	3	4	186	209
Glacier Bay NP & PRES	4,499,148	1,062,623	79	104	6,507	8,310
Glacier NP	12,521,600	2,872,611	310	387	17,757	22,343
Glen Canyon NRA	8,670,047	2,338,753	184	212	11,927	13,783
Golden Gate NRA	14,870,743	3,635,181	273	346	22,378	29,417
Golden Spike NHS	583,982	161,466	13	16	835	1,004
Governors Island NM	662,689	152,418	13	16	973	1,256
Grand Canyon NP	26,843,707	7,310,659	584	671	37,069	42,919
Grand Portage NM	727,313	190,453	17	20	996	1,160
Grand Teton NP	11,483,430	2,949,919	264	310	15,862	18,850
Grant-Kohrs Ranch NHS	966,425	269,430	23	29	1,431	1,798
Great Basin NP	2,142,767	557,479	50	53	2,782	3,024
Great Sand Dunes NP & PRES	1,501,867	435,452	32	38	2,115	2,455
Great Smoky Mountains NP	15,245,723	4,447,249	345	406	21,589	25,557
Greenbelt Park	777,027	176,820	16	19	1,092	1,347
Guadalupe Mountains NP	1,921,908	545,501	48	53	2,607	2,910
Guilford Courthouse NMP	576,041	170,266	14	18	893	1,158
Gulf Islands NS	5,379,089	1,426,352	119	151	7,803	9,757
Hagerman Fossil Beds NM	450,793	122,917	10	12	635	757
Haleakala NP	4,234,717	1,067,594	103	126	6,150	7,796
Hamilton Grange NMEM	89,568	27,538	2	3	138	177
Hampton NHS	950,918	233,495	27	31	1,329	1,603
Harpers Ferry NHP	5,069,979	1,430,814	116	135	7,245	8,699
Harry S Truman NHS	868,404	257,938	20	28	1,491	2,101
Hawaii Volcanoes NP	7,700,300	1,993,211	163	213	11,325	14,475
Herbert Hoover NHS	900,408	223,127	21	27	1,303	1,643
Home of Franklin D. Roosevelt NHS	1,093,821	294,076	27	32	1,585	1,961
Homestead National Monument of America	879,381	256,348	22	28	1,306	1,621
Hopewell Culture NHP	737,445	159,776	18	21	998	1,198

Table A-2. Payroll Impacts of National Park Units on Local Economies, FY 2009 (continued)

Park Unit	Park Payroll			Impacts of Park Payroll		
	Salary	Payroll Benefits	NPS Jobs	Total Jobs	Labor Income ($000's)	Value Added ($000's)
Hopewell Furnace NHS	1,111,965	273,867	21	28	1,636	2,102
Horseshoe Bend NMP	516,125	144,444	12	15	731	872
Hot Springs NP	3,100,565	873,230	71	88	4,423	5,303
Hovenweep NM	363,107	117,580	7	9	527	621
Hubbell Trading Post NHS	671,573	151,241	13	14	853	938
Independence NHP	11,893,785	3,303,503	218	291	18,800	25,240
Indiana Dunes NL	6,281,485	1,771,447	125	162	9,262	11,568
Isle Royale NP	3,147,724	717,326	64	78	4,244	5,006
James A. Garfield NHS	359,814	94,253	9	11	528	662
Jean Lafitte NHP & PRES	3,322,403	953,149	74	92	4,990	6,316
Jefferson National Expansion Memorial	8,009,618	2,372,199	191	232	11,916	14,760
Jewel Cave NM	875,889	186,831	25	30	1,234	1,553
Jimmy Carter NHS	913,313	291,944	22	26	1,310	1,527
John D Rockefeller Jr. MEM PKWY	349,101	109,967	6	7	502	590
John Day Fossil Beds NM	1,026,044	260,289	24	26	1,330	1,426
John F. Kennedy NHS	292,480	74,153	5	7	443	575
John Muir NHS	665,368	179,031	14	17	993	1,269
Johnstown Flood NMEM	469,704	149,487	9	12	713	888
Joshua Tree NP	5,518,494	1,495,340	127	145	7,711	9,076
Kalaupapa NHP	2,376,934	645,007	47	60	3,498	4,421
Kaloko-Honokohau NHP	1,191,089	338,334	29	37	1,782	2,269
Katmai NP & PRES/Aniakchak NM & PRES	2,442,606	549,096	43	43	2,992	2,992
Kenai Fjords NP	2,210,793	481,679	47	59	3,157	4,043
Kennesaw Mountain NBP	984,484	266,531	19	25	1,510	1,989
Kings Mountain NMP	750,197	189,938	18	22	1,047	1,257
Klondike Gold Rush NHP Alaska	2,195,523	494,602	40	52	3,151	4,031
Klondike Gold Rush NHP Seattle	405,547	114,873	13	15	635	847
Knife River Indian Villages NHS	569,474	157,615	13	17	844	1,056
Lake Clark NP & PRES	1,646,564	410,560	30	39	2,403	3,063
Lake Mead NRA	16,207,935	4,368,172	379	425	22,365	25,849
Lake Meredith NRA	2,144,373	654,967	53	56	2,919	3,110
Lake Roosevelt NRA	3,238,907	824,078	73	89	4,544	5,474
Lassen Volcanic NP	4,237,927	1,016,514	90	114	6,107	7,674
Lava Beds NM	1,830,118	490,228	43	49	2,532	2,941
LBJ Memorial Grove on the Potomac	25,733	7,376	2	3	38	46
Lewis & Clark NHP	1,100,217	273,312	29	32	1,470	1,669
Lincoln Boyhood NMEM	613,633	165,558	15	18	862	1,030
Lincoln Home NHS	2,083,722	518,926	51	61	2,942	3,560
Little Bighorn Battlefield NM	922,995	227,811	22	28	1,337	1,686

Table A-2. Payroll Impacts of National Park Units on Local Economies, FY 2009 (continued)

Park Unit	Park Payroll			Impacts of Park Payroll		
	Salary	Payroll Benefits	NPS Jobs	Total Jobs	Labor Income ($000's)	Value Added ($000's)
Little River Canyon NPRES	860,193	252,916	20	25	1,246	1,508
Little Rock Central High School NHS	500,568	124,173	10	13	721	893
Longfellow NHS	807,055	188,376	16	19	1,162	1,470
Lowell NHP	5,567,845	1,371,249	105	130	8,089	10,211
Lyndon B. Johnson NHP	2,426,394	687,084	55	65	3,518	4,284
Maggie L Walker NHS	458,771	117,088	11	13	679	868
Mammoth Cave NP	6,170,575	1,404,935	178	205	8,409	9,979
Manassas NBP	1,894,070	515,632	32	38	2,693	3,259
Manzanar NHS	801,047	194,522	17	19	1,046	1,163
Marsh-Billings-Rockefeller NHP	1,223,269	268,618	27	34	1,752	2,232
Martin Luther King, Jr. NHS	1,836,657	415,590	35	43	2,605	3,255
Martin Van Buren NHS	794,826	181,091	16	19	1,103	1,331
Mary McLeod Bethune Council House NHS	447,460	104,164	10	12	631	778
Mesa Verde NP	5,449,208	1,314,773	130	152	7,521	9,005
Minute Man NHP	1,993,640	490,868	41	50	2,896	3,656
Missouri National Recreational River	448,288	108,321	10	12	601	693
Mojave NPRES	3,592,918	1,053,408	69	85	5,392	6,736
Monocacy NB	1,161,961	347,092	25	29	1,706	2,089
Montezuma Castle NM	1,364,853	385,271	31	41	2,138	2,850
Moores Creek NB	222,492	64,266	5	7	327	407
Morristown NHP	1,665,951	424,248	35	42	2,442	3,097
Mount Rainier NP	10,299,687	2,296,200	243	293	14,488	18,004
Mount Rushmore NMEM	3,712,752	999,885	90	113	5,447	6,812
Muir Woods NM	585,126	149,818	13	16	878	1,140
Natchez NHP	893,195	275,631	20	22	1,216	1,341
Natchez Trace PKWY	7,184,044	2,396,950	152	174	10,209	11,512
National Capital Parks-Central	13,898,613	3,469,315	294	342	19,845	24,400
National Capital Parks-East	7,725,635	2,039,544	150	177	11,142	13,674
Natural Bridges NM	348,119	89,136	8	8	456	504
Navajo NM	646,538	134,394	16	18	851	992
New Bedford Whaling NHP	408,880	98,325	9	11	600	773
New Orleans Jazz NHP	288,103	92,987	7	9	443	558
New River Gorge NR	5,337,040	1,634,102	113	113	6,971	6,971
Nez Perce NHP	1,732,026	475,560	37	46	2,471	2,969
Nicodemus NHS	257,703	77,600	6	6	335	335
Ninety Six NHS	342,333	89,067	10	11	474	562
Niobrara NSR	485,134	152,071	10	13	685	785
North Cascades NP	6,663,772	1,787,412	158	195	10,177	13,390
Obed Wild and Scenic River	446,714	132,246	9	11	637	751
Ocmulgee NM	732,264	153,068	18	22	1,024	1,284

Table A-2. Payroll Impacts of National Park Units on Local Economies, FY 2009 (continued)

Park Unit	Park Payroll			Impacts of Park Payroll		
	Salary	Payroll Benefits	NPS Jobs	Total Jobs	Labor Income ($000's)	Value Added ($000's)
Olympic NP	10,860,889	2,666,175	239	288	15,042	18,092
Oregon Caves NM	1,036,519	228,552	26	32	1,455	1,805
Organ Pipe Cactus NM	2,372,589	743,245	44	61	3,807	5,076
Ozark National Scenic Riverways	4,856,832	1,419,557	103	129	7,071	8,389
Padre Island NS	3,300,551	792,177	77	97	4,768	5,992
Palo Alto Battlefield NHP	477,377	143,044	11	14	708	870
Pea Ridge NMP	968,374	256,886	28	33	1,349	1,600
Pecos NHP	1,393,337	423,878	29	39	2,158	2,784
Perry's Victory and International Peace MEM	870,806	240,466	20	25	1,288	1,610
Petersburg NB	2,202,738	591,951	42	55	3,225	4,083
Petrified Forest NP	2,615,955	696,888	54	62	3,577	4,132
Petroglyph NM	1,272,955	307,602	29	39	1,914	2,529
Pictured Rocks NL	1,675,001	370,556	34	34	2,060	2,117
Pinnacles NM	2,308,236	604,675	48	56	3,287	4,013
Pipe Spring NM	715,826	182,411	17	20	1,009	1,221
Pipestone NM	533,685	123,301	15	19	782	1,014
Piscataway Park	7,725,635	2,039,544	150	177	11,142	13,674
Point Reyes NS	6,627,521	1,787,002	129	160	10,039	12,994
Prince William Forest Park	1,993,217	607,680	42	49	2,956	3,609
Pu'uhonua o Honaunau NHP	1,162,760	321,980	28	35	1,731	2,207
Puukohola Heiau NHS	898,003	197,052	21	27	1,285	1,653
Rainbow Bridge NM	73,863	18,866	2	2	101	116
Redwood NP	6,699,121	1,838,607	141	169	9,421	11,106
Richmond NBP	1,855,909	526,294	41	51	2,798	3,565
Rio Grande Wild and Scenic River	116,817	58,480	2	3	185	208
Rock Creek Park	3,734,163	939,574	87	100	5,339	6,563
Rocky Mountain NP	13,723,833	3,442,917	324	394	19,713	24,615
Roger Williams NMEM	326,495	93,085	8	10	522	703
Russell Cave NM	222,357	50,309	7	7	300	355
Sagamore Hill NHS	1,158,536	291,290	27	32	1,719	2,209
Saguaro NP	3,169,689	893,045	82	96	4,519	5,387
Saint Croix NSR	2,725,335	718,612	59	75	4,037	5,131
Saint-Gaudens NHS	864,005	221,621	17	22	1,232	1,522
Salem Maritime NHS	1,942,962	463,935	48	56	2,732	3,349
Salinas Pueblo Missions NM	1,042,509	243,317	30	39	1,559	2,065
San Antonio Missions NHP	2,297,323	734,589	53	67	3,567	4,560
San Francisco Maritime NHP	5,753,703	1,506,341	89	109	8,449	10,649
San Juan Island NHP	670,452	167,545	15	18	919	1,078
San Juan NHS	3,588,932	840,828	109	125	4,944	5,838
Santa Monica Mountains NRA	5,559,259	1,574,251	122	147	8,300	10,408

Table A-2. Payroll Impacts of National Park Units on Local Economies, FY 2009 (continued)

Park Unit	Park Payroll			Impacts of Park Payroll		
	Salary	Payroll Benefits	NPS Jobs	Total Jobs	Labor Income ($000's)	Value Added ($000's)
Saratoga NHP	1,306,382	358,677	29	33	1,822	2,126
Saugus Iron Works NHS	578,438	149,836	13	16	874	1,128
Scotts Bluff NM	663,331	170,846	17	20	934	1,118
Sequoia NP/ Kings Canyon NP	15,722,306	3,879,539	374	442	22,081	26,747
Shenandoah NP	9,919,997	2,855,440	228	283	14,752	18,158
Shiloh NMP	1,530,352	393,632	37	45	2,131	2,557
Sitka NHP	1,361,599	329,938	28	35	1,978	2,523
Sleeping Bear Dunes NL	3,726,444	740,602	83	108	5,316	6,922
Springfield Armory NHS	861,531	195,666	16	21	1,290	1,710
Statue of Liberty NM	9,097,865	2,188,968	189	224	13,454	17,342
Steamtown NHS	3,586,149	1,036,761	64	88	5,484	7,020
Stones River NB	1,208,443	255,104	30	38	1,820	2,448
Tallgrass Prairie NPRES	675,684	169,799	16	18	893	994
Thaddeus Kosciuszko NMEM	114,865	40,898	3	4	191	253
Theodore Roosevelt Birthplace NHS	187,774	54,771	5	6	287	368
Theodore Roosevelt Island Park	66,534	20,900	2	2	99	121
Theodore Roosevelt NP	2,054,004	551,591	55	66	2,917	3,498
Thomas Edison NHP	1,655,722	410,551	34	41	2,429	3,097
Thomas Stone NHS	221,619	36,262	8	9	287	348
Timpanogos Cave NM	1,172,951	232,195	42	50	1,698	2,230
Tonto NM	636,800	181,071	13	18	1,009	1,362
Tumacacori NHP	1,006,555	268,445	20	25	1,438	1,746
Tuskegee Airmen NHS	405,156	98,070	13	15	548	643
Tuskegee Institute NHS	473,125	108,796	11	13	635	746
Tuzigoot NM	17,623	4,159	1	1	27	36
Ulysses S. Grant NHS	615,926	147,268	19	22	881	1,100
Upper Delaware SRR	2,069,292	508,227	36	44	2,829	3,358
USS Arizona Memorial	1,814,760	459,134	42	55	2,784	3,714
Valley Forge NHP	4,573,460	1,243,673	77	105	7,193	9,651
Vanderbilt Mansion NHS	869,606	195,876	25	29	1,222	1,521
Vicksburg NMP	1,937,915	521,945	49	59	2,786	3,383
Virgin Islands NP	3,211,780	878,498	70	84	4,551	5,351
Voyageurs NP	3,419,330	925,911	70	88	4,931	5,996
Washita Battlefield NHS	352,977	113,270	10	12	503	580
Weir Farm NHS	746,735	194,404	14	17	1,079	1,340
Whiskeytown-Shasta-Trinity NRA	3,558,926	953,617	93	112	5,155	6,331
White House	5,991,783	1,462,053	125	146	8,522	10,485
White Sands NM	1,124,072	300,904	28	32	1,522	1,730
Whitman Mission NHS	568,157	136,418	11	14	793	957
William Howard Taft NHS	487,704	139,495	9	12	739	938

Table A-2. Payroll Impacts of National Park Units on Local Economies, FY 2009 (continued)

Park Unit	Park Payroll			Impacts of Park Payroll		
	Salary	Payroll Benefits	NPS Jobs	Total Jobs	Labor Income ($000's)	Value Added ($000's)
Wilson's Creek NB	1,590,327	429,461	35	47	2,390	3,059
Wind Cave NP	3,161,867	867,056	83	98	4,610	5,689
Wolf Trap NP for the Performing Arts	2,765,905	617,599	67	76	3,877	4,783
Women's Rights NHP	932,734	249,282	18	22	1,315	1,574
Wrangell-St Elias NP & PRES	3,753,084	721,511	68	88	5,263	6,767
Wright Brothers NMEM	396,676	88,741	10	13	563	719
Wupatki NM	2,404,585	611,873	51	60	3,320	3,911
Yellowstone NP	29,735,534	7,863,220	662	786	41,461	49,474
Yosemite NP	37,756,060	9,282,227	922	1,031	50,684	58,133
Yukon-Charley Rivers NPRES	1,220,787	283,954	33	40	1,761	2,250
Zion NP	8,418,948	2,270,333	211	265	12,203	15,059

Notes: Jobs include part-time and full-time jobs with seasonal positions adjusted to an annual basis. NPS jobs, salary, and benefits are assigned to the unit where the employee's time was charged, which may differ from their duty station. Economic impacts include NPS payroll and jobs plus the induced effects of NPS employee spending of their wages and salaries in the local region.

Table A-3. Payroll Impacts of National Park Units on Local Economies, Administrative Units and Parks without Visit Counts, FY 2009

Park Unit	Park Payroll			Impacts of Park Payroll		
	Salary	Payroll Benefits	NPS Jobs	Total Jobs	Labor Income ($000's)	Value Added ($000's)
Administration Team Coord, PGSO	10,354,541	2,323,772	159	213	15,150	17,208
Ala Kahakai NHT	158,403	47,197	2	3	226	245
Alaska Regional Office	4,629,810	1,024,094	65	90	6,586	7,400
Alaska Support Office	9,862,732	2,159,416	159	190	12,884	13,811
American Memorial Park	572,252	167,064	14	16	812	883
Anchorage Interagency Visitors Center	436,893	71,892	10	12	597	674
Appalachian NST	753,965	201,879	10	14	1,108	1,240
Associate Reg Dir, Administration	9,258,881	2,189,753	143	195	13,312	14,941
Biological Resources Mgmt Division	1,890,663	478,990	26	37	2,750	3,083
Blackstone River Valley NHC	741,263	209,780	13	17	1,100	1,231
Boston Harbor Islands NRA	790,277	159,749	18	22	1,109	1,248
Boston Support Office	897,639	220,327	12	17	1,299	1,457
Cedar Creek and Belle Grove NHP	192,962	39,230	2	3	278	317
Center For Urban Ecology	269,526	66,070	7	8	390	437
Chesapeake Bay Program Office	1,153,855	308,515	17	24	1,695	1,898
Chihuahuan Desert Network	207,255	65,083	3	5	314	351
Columbia Cascades So	5,426,292	1,362,297	80	109	8,084	9,163
Denver Service Center	20,616,057	5,210,418	471	585	29,976	33,603
Ebey's Landing NHRES	273,953	72,442	6	7	381	415
Erie Canalway NHC	251,763	72,322	7	8	356	387
Fairbanks Interagency Visitors Center	365,350	84,186	10	11	496	541
Flagstaff Areas	1,232	124	3	3	2	2
FLETC (Fed Law Enforcement Tng Ctr)	1,860,272	636,648	70	81	2,871	3,199
Glen Echo Park	295,686	85,543	8	9	419	455
Gloria Dei Church NHS	25,046	7,266	2	2	36	39
Great Falls Park	744,693	193,921	19	23	1,088	1,220
Great Lakes Network	706,208	193,089	17	21	1,041	1,166
Greater Yellowstone Network	393,179	102,030	7	10	574	644
Harpers Ferry Center	9,222,555	2,223,750	169	207	12,621	13,755
Heartland Network	487,503	153,829	10	13	739	825
Historic Preservation Training Ctr (HPTC)	2,531,697	627,480	60	73	3,669	4,114
Horace Albright Training Ctr	1,008,894	260,091	16	22	1,472	1,650
Ice Age NST	330,233	81,631	7	8	454	495
Intermountain Nr-Pro	868,875	218,333	20	25	1,262	1,415
Intermountain Regional Office	22,187,720	5,276,223	344	466	31,929	35,833
Keweenaw NHP	1,112,428	262,305	26	30	1,472	1,577
Land Acquisition Project Office	393,142	99,203	5	7	586	664
Lewis & Clark NHT	963,981	299,212	17	21	1,386	1,505
Manhattan Sites	993,349	270,404	18	24	1,464	1,638

Table A-3. Payroll Impacts of National Park Units on Local Economies, Administrative Units and Parks without Visit Counts, FY 2009 (continued)

Park Unit	Park Payroll			Impacts of Park Payroll		
	Salary	Payroll Benefits	NPS Jobs	Total Jobs	Labor Income ($000's)	Value Added ($000's)
Mather Training Ctr	930,576	231,424	14	19	1,349	1,513
Midwest Archeological Center	1,470,625	349,313	32	40	2,171	2,463
Midwest Regional Office	13,889,952	3,619,634	206	282	20,305	22,749
Minidoka Internment NM	160,411	41,769	6	6	223	242
Mississippi NR&RA	1,606,264	425,662	33	41	2,415	2,735
Museum Resources Ctr	543,144	125,428	8	11	778	873
National Capital Regional Office	3,621,499	824,331	78	98	5,175	5,812
National Interagency Fire Center	4,091,184	1,195,005	61	82	6,263	7,076
National Mall	4,427,568	1,045,392	99	123	6,364	7,143
National Parks Of New York Harbor	566,346	120,489	8	11	801	900
National Trails System, Santa Fe	1,432,509	389,627	22	30	2,164	2,449
Natl Ctr For Rec & Conservation	1,211,389	316,969	15	22	1,772	1,985
NER Historic Architecture Program	691,084	149,374	12	15	1,005	1,143
North Country NST	304,816	75,909	6	8	453	514
Northeast Education Services Center	122,768	36,591	1	2	189	213
Northeast Museum Services Center	814,259	225,594	14	18	1,234	1,396
Northeast Regional Office	20,930,160	4,904,373	298	408	30,830	34,991
Northern Colorado Plateau Network	759,843	219,208	17	21	1,132	1,266
Northern Great Plains Network	319,840	94,680	7	9	479	535
NP Of American Samoa	822,525	185,784	20	23	1,113	1,214
Office Of The Chief Information Officer	7,422,718	1,801,349	77	118	10,718	12,024
Office Of The Director	79,848,520	19,243,638	1,150	1,591	115,162	129,210
Office Of Wyoming State Coordinator	106,783	25,410	1	2	158	179
Old Post Office Tower	365,117	103,526	8	10	542	606
Olmstead Center For Landscape Preservation	760,084	214,211	16	20	1,156	1,307
Overmountain Victory NHT	80,079	15,981	1	2	115	131
Pacific Island Support Office	837,866	190,275	11	16	1,228	1,395
Pacific West Regional Office	8,870,699	2,048,323	155	202	13,036	14,800
Parashant NM	652,418	178,293	12	15	986	1,116
Pinelands NRES (Interp Pgm)	147,395	40,485	3	3	223	252
Potomac Heritage NST	117,882	36,672	3	4	178	199
Presidio Of San Francisco	8,161,022	2,428,719	148	193	12,232	13,668
Rocky Mountain Network	428,887	113,653	7	10	629	704
Roosevelt-Vanderbilt Headquarters	1,879,037	482,961	31	42	2,740	3,071
Rosie the Riveter WW II Home Front NHP	546,345	126,913	10	13	783	879
Saint Croix Island International HS	189,879	35,901	4	5	271	309
Salt River Bay NHP & Ecological PRES	339,730	89,335	8	9	510	578
Sand Creek Massacre NHS	328,223	88,284	10	11	495	560
SE Archeological Center	1,556,256	364,635	35	43	2,292	2,602

Table A-3. Payroll Impacts of National Park Units on Local Economies, Administrative Units and Parks without Visit Counts, FY 2009 (continued)

	Park Payroll			Impacts of Park Payroll		
Park Unit	Salary	Payroll Benefits	NPS Jobs	Total Jobs	Labor Income ($000's)	Value Added ($000's)
Selma To Montgomery NHT	198,437	46,119	8	9	292	331
Sonoran Desert Network	502,582	156,084	11	13	760	848
Southeast Regional Office	16,244,085	4,295,007	234	320	24,416	27,646
Southern Arizona Group	567,432	152,056	10	13	855	968
Southern Colorado Plateau Network	636,732	201,481	11	14	966	1,078
Southern Plains Network	210,401	50,240	3	5	303	340
Spanish Colonial Research Center	107,542	35,397	2	3	169	190
Strategic Planning Division	285,988	71,887	3	5	415	466
United States Park Police	64,380,961	22,578,493	988	1,343	99,916	111,243
Virgin Islands Coral Reef NM	161,498	56,913	6	7	257	289
Washington Training Ctr	476,816	87,470	6	8	660	744
Western Archeological & Conservation Center	552,290	133,342	13	15	817	927
Western Arctic National Parklands	1,637,761	363,559	27	36	2,392	2,718
Yucca House NM	69,899	24,894	3	3	111	125

Notes: Jobs include part-time and full-time jobs with seasonal positions adjusted to an annual basis. NPS jobs, salary, and benefits are assigned to the unit where the employee's time was charged, which may differ from their duty station. Economic impacts include NPS payroll and jobs plus the induced effects of NPS employee spending of their wages and salaries in the local region.

Table A-4. Impacts of NPS Visitor Spending and Payroll on Local Economies by State, 2009

State	Recreation Visits	Non-Local Visitor Spending ($000's)	Jobs from Non-Local Visitor Spending	Payroll-related Jobs	Total Jobs
Alabama	790,752	18,781	303	96	399
Alaska	2,278,474	216,224	3,039	1,072	4,111
American Samoa				39	39
Arizona	10,713,122	659,180	8,911	1,336	10,247
Arkansas	3,031,842	129,498	2,043	328	2,371
California	35,023,586	1,054,833	13,357	4,073	17,430
Colorado	5,443,039	336,956	4,900	1,893	6,793
Connecticut	19,386	1,130	13	17	29
District of Columbia	35,695,833	966,189	11,310	5,126	16,436
Florida	9,495,437	552,809	8,093	931	9,024
Georgia	6,475,874	199,024	2,736	672	3,408
Guam	271,608	8,521	98		98
Hawaii	4,312,818	222,157	2,930	556	3,487
Idaho	494,196	17,952	269	172	442
Illinois	464,074	23,166	373	61	434
Indiana	2,230,024	51,232	753	197	950
Iowa	241,063	11,494	198	60	257
Kansas	101,906	4,337	74	88	162
Kentucky	1,630,944	76,593	1,265	321	1,586
Louisiana	443,314	19,869	281	118	399
Maine	2,227,698	159,106	2,763	198	2,960
Maryland	3,445,530	155,549	2,035	537	2,572
Massachusetts	9,772,738	384,992	5,102	723	5,824
Michigan	1,628,704	124,132	2,130	250	2,380
Minnesota	650,156	27,990	453	205	658
Mississippi	6,582,890	76,254	1,086	258	1,344
Missouri	3,933,043	142,684	2,096	476	2,572
Montana	4,455,469	269,523	4,031	886	4,917
Nebraska	273,444	8,763	167	133	301
Nevada	5,836,491	173,140	1,845	387	2,232
New Hampshire	34,558	1,176	19	22	40
New Jersey	5,828,477	94,657	1,144	282	1,427
New Mexico	1,659,574	62,474	909	543	1,452
New York	17,327,234	340,054	3,820	1,016	4,836
North Carolina	18,198,530	707,241	10,317	636	10,953
North Dakota	631,459	27,545	487	98	585
Ohio	2,882,593	56,716	875	324	1,199
Oklahoma	1,249,011	12,670	170	98	268
Oregon	891,783	51,375	798	207	1,005
Pennsylvania	8,885,894	295,605	4,325	1,277	5,602
Puerto Rico	1,069,673	47,942	683	125	808
Rhode Island	50,397	2,936	46	10	57
South Carolina	1,504,680	40,265	627	128	755
South Dakota	4,134,663	141,846	2,201	351	2,552
Tennessee	7,777,790	501,305	7,265	447	7,712
Texas	6,938,238	247,074	3,690	677	4,367
Utah	8,755,401	565,592	8,551	897	9,448

Table A-4. Impacts of NPS Visitor Spending and Payroll on Local Economies by State, 2009 (continued)

State	Recreation Visits	Non-Local Visitor Spending ($000's)	Jobs from Non-Local Visitor Spending	Payroll-related Jobs	Total Jobs
Vermont	31,129	1,395	20	34	54
Virgin Islands	577,931	56,572	966	122	1,088
Virginia	22,953,894	493,128	6,806	1,192	7,998
Washington	7,559,552	247,832	3,679	962	4,641
West Virginia	1,803,552	57,779	720	478	1,198
Wisconsin	452,365	25,044	412	112	523
Wyoming	6,117,188	570,480	8,523	808	9,331
Total	**285,279,020**	**10,740,784**	**149,706**	**32,056**	**181,762**

Notes: Payroll-related jobs include NPS jobs and the induced effects of the NPS payroll on the local economy, covering parks with visit counts (Table A-2) as well as administrative units and parks without visit counts (Table A-3). Total job impacts include those supported by non-local visitor spending and the NPS payroll. For 20 parks with property in more than one state, activity is allocated using the proportions in Table A-6.

Table A-5. Impacts of NPS Visitor Spending and Payroll on Local Economies by Region, 2009

Region	Recreation Visits	Non-Local Spending ($ Millions)	Jobs from Non-Local Visitor Spending	Payroll-related Jobs	Total Jobs
Alaska	2,278,474	216,224	3,039	1,072	4,110
Harpers Ferry				207	207
Intermountain	42,882,594	2,647,522	38,816	7,018	45,834
Midwest	20,644,870	773,839	12,250	2,684	14,935
National Capital	47,717,757	1,166,805	13,682	2,173	15,856
Northeast	54,240,906	1,674,460	22,857	4,556	27,413
Pacific West	56,357,028	1,833,863	23,602	6,504	30,105
Southeast	61,157,391	2,428,072	35,459	3,975	39,434
Washington Office				3,868	3,868
Total	**285,279,020**	**10,740,784**	**149,705**	**32,056**	**181,762**

Notes: Payroll-related jobs include NPS jobs and the induced effects of the NPS payroll on the local economy, covering parks with visit counts (Table A-2) as well as administrative units and parks without visit counts (Table A-3). Total job impacts include those supported by non-local visitor spending and the NPS payroll.

Table A-6. Allocations to States for Multi-state Parks

Park	State	Share
Assateague Island NS	MD	33%
Assateague Island NS	VA	67%
Bighorn Canyon NRA	WY	46%
Bighorn Canyon NRA	MT	54%
Big South Fork NRRA	KY	41%
Big South Fork NRRA	TN	59%
Blue Ridge Parkway	VA	38%
Blue Ridge Parkway	NC	62%
Chickamauga & Chattanooga NMP	GA	50%
Chickamauga & Chattanooga NMP	TN	50%
Chesapeake & Ohio Canal NHP	WV	6%
Chesapeake & Ohio Canal NHP	MD	9%
Chesapeake & Ohio Canal NHP	DC	85%
Cumberland Gap NHP	KY	93%
Cumberland Gap NHP	VA	7%
Delaware Water Gap NRA	PA	29%
Delaware Water Gap NRA	NJ	71%
Dinosaur NM	UT	26%
Dinosaur NM	CO	74%
Gateway NRA	NJ	20%
Gateway NRA	NY	80%
Glen Canyon NRA	AZ	8%
Glen Canyon NRA	UT	92%
Great Smoky Mountains NP	NC	44%
Great Smoky Mountains NP	TN	56%
Gulf Islands Nat Seashore	MS	25%
Gulf Islands Nat Seashore	FL	75%
Hovenweep NM	CO	44%
Hovenweep NM	UT	56%
Lake Mead NRA	AZ	25%
Lake Mead NRA	NV	75%
Natchez Trace Parkway	AL	7%
Natchez Trace Parkway	TN	13%
Natchez Trace Parkway	MS	80%
National capital Parks East	MD	10%
National capital Parks East	DC	90%
Saint Croix Nat scenic river	MN	50%
Saint Croix Nat scenic river	WI	50%
Upper Delaware SRR	NY	50%
Upper Delaware SRR	PA	50%
Yellowstone NP	WY	49%
Yellowstone NP	MT	51%

The Department of the Interior protects and manages the nation's natural resources and cultural heritage; provides scientific and other information about those resources; and honors its special responsibilities to American Indians, Alaska Natives, and affiliated Island Communities.

NPS 999/106327, January 2011

www.ingramcontent.com/pod-product-compliance
Lightning Source LLC
Chambersburg PA
CBHW081624170526
45166CB00009B/3096